# FIREBIRD

## RED BOOK

Peter C. Sessler

*Special thanks to Bruce Bartlett, Don Keefe, Bart Orlans and Pontiac Public Relations.*

First published in 1992 by Motorbooks International Publishers & Wholesalers, P O Box 2, 729 Prospect Avenue, Osceola, WI 54020 USA

Library of Congress Cataloging-in-Publication Data
Sessler, Peter C.
    Firebird red book / Peter C. Sessler.
      p.   cm. — (Motorbooks International red book series)
    Includes index.
    ISBN 0-87938-568-5
    1. Firebird automobile—History.   I. Title.   II. Series.
TL215.F57S47  1992
629.222′2—dc20        91-30438

**On the front cover:** The 1973 Pontiac Firebird SD-455 owned by Jack Janney. *Tim Parker*

Printed and bound in the United States of America

# Contents

# Introduction

*Firebird Red Book* is designed to help the Pontiac enthusiast determine the authenticity and originality of any Firebird built between 1967 and 1992. Each chapter covers a model year; included are production figures, serial numbers, engine codes, carburetor numbers, distributor numbers, head casting numbers, exterior color codes, interior trim codes, convertible and vinyl top color codes, option codes and prices, and selected facts. Not all engines are covered in the same detail because of space limitations.

For the enthusiast, the most important number in any Firebird is its vehicle identification number (VIN). From 1967 to 1971, it consisted of a thirteen-digit number that broke down to model year, body style and series, assembly plant and consecutive sequence number. In 1972, Pontiac—as well as the rest of General Motors—adopted a new VIN system, still using thirteen digits but, most important, including a number code identifying the engine the car was equipped with. Until 1971, you could not tell which engine came in a particular car, only whether the car was equipped with a six- or eight-cylinder engine. Pontiac stamped the last eight digits of the car's VIN on the engine, thereby "matching" the engine to the car. Unfortunately, it is easy to restamp a cylinder block with the VIN, thereby increasing a car's value. See the appendix for engine identification and cowl tag information that is designed to help you determine authenticity.

From 1981, in an industrywide move, all manufacturers used the same seventeen-digit numbering system, which included even more information.

The car's VIN was stamped on a metal plate and attached to the driver's-side door pillar until 1967. From 1968 on, the number was stamped on a plate and attached to the left side of the dash, making it visible through the windshield.

Even if all the numbers match on a particular car you are looking at, especially on one built before 1972, it would be to your advantage if the car is documented. It is all the better if the previous owner can provide you with the original invoice or window sticker, any service records or the car's broadcast sheet. The broadcast sheet—usually located under the seats, under the carpets or behind the dash—is a factory computer print-out showing what options a car was built with. This is especially important with the rare, popular models, such as the SD 455 Trans Am and Formulas.

The colors and interior trim listed in each chapter are correct as far as they go. However, Pontiac did build cars in colors and trim combinations not listed. As with all the information given here, be open to the possibility that exceptions can and do occur. This means that you'll have to work harder to determine authenticity.

Although every effort has been made to make sure that the information contained in this book is correct, I cannot assume any responsibility for any loss arising from the use of this book. However, I would like to hear from any enthusiast with corrections or interesting additions. Please write to me care of Motorbooks International.

# Chapter 1

# 1967 Firebird

## Production

| | |
|---|---|
| 2 dr coupe 6 cyl | 17,664 |
| 2 dr convertible 8 cyl | 64,896 |
| Total | 82,560 |

## Serial Numbers

**Description**

223377U100001

22337—model number (22337 = 2 dr coupe, 22367 = 2 dr convertible)

7—last digit of model year (7 = 1967)

U—assembly plant (L = Lordstown)

100001—consecutive sequence number (100001 = 8 cyl, 600001 = 6 cyl)

**Location**

On plate attached to left front door hinge post.

## Engine Identification Codes

ZK—230 ci I-6 1 bbl 165 hp manual
ZN—230 ci I-6 1 bbl 165 hp automatic
ZD—230 ci I-6 4 bbl 215 hp manual
ZE—230 ci I-6 4 bbl 215 hp automatic
WC—326 ci V-8 2 bbl 250 hp manual
WH—326 ci V-8 2 bbl 250 hp manual w/AIR
YJ—326 ci V-8 2 bbl 250 hp automatic
XI—326 ci V-8 2 bbl 250 hp automatic w/AIR
WK—326 ci V-8 4 bbl 285 hp manual
WO—326 ci V-8 4 bbl 285 hp manual w/AIR
YM—326 ci V-8 4 bbl 285 hp automatic
XO—326 ci V-8 4 bbl 285 hp automatic w/AIR
WZ—400 ci V-8 4 bbl 325 hp manual
WU—400 ci V-8 4 bbl 325 hp manual w/AIR
YT—400 ci V-8 4 bbl 325 hp automatic
WI—400 ci V-8 4 bbl 325 hp manual Ram Air
WQ—400 ci V-8 4 bbl 325 hp manual Ram Air w/AIR
XN—400 ci V-8 4 bbl 325 hp automatic Ram Air

## Carburetors

326 ci 250 hp manual—7027071
326 ci 250 hp manual w/AIR—7037071
326 ci 250 hp automatic—7027062
326 ci 250 hp automatic w/AIR—7037062
326 ci 285 hp manual—Carter AFB4234S

326 ci 285 hp manual w/AIR—Carter AFB4245S
326 ci 285 hp automatic—Carter AFB4246S
326 ci 285 hp automatic w/AIR—Carter AFB4248S
400 ci 325 hp manual—7027273
400 ci 325 hp manual w/AIR—7037273
400 ci 325 hp manual Ram Air—7027277
400 ci 325 hp manual Ram Air w/AIR—7037277
400 ci 325 hp automatic—7027272
400 ci 325 hp automatic Ram Air—7027276

## Distributors

326 ci 250 hp—1111164,
   1111199
326 ci 285 hp—1111165,
   1111238
400 ci 325 hp—1111250,
   1111252, 1111253, 1111254

## Head Castings

326 ci 250 hp—140
326 ci 285 hp—141
400 ci 325 hp—670
400 ci 325 hp Ram Air—670
   w/AIR
400 ci 325 hp Ram Air—670,
   97

## Exterior Color Codes

| | | | |
|---|---|---|---|
| Starlight Black | A | Mariner Turquoise | L |
| Cameo Ivory | C | Plum Mist | M |
| Montreaux Blue | D | Burgundy | N |
| Fathom Blue | E | Silverglaze | P |
| Tyrol Blue | F | Regimental Red | R |
| Signet Gold | G | Champagne | S |
| Linden Green | H | Montego Cream | T |
| Gulf Turquoise | K | | |

## Interior Trim Codes

| Color | Std Interior | Custom Interior* |
|---|---|---|
| Blue | 250 | 255 |
| Gold | 251 | 257 |
| Red | 252 | 258 |
| Black | 253 | 259 |
| Parchment | 254 | 260 |
| Turquoise | — | 256 |

*Available with exterior color codes C and F.

## Convertible Top Color Codes

| | |
|---|---|
| Ivory | 1 |
| Black | 2 |
| Blue | 4 |
| Turquoise | 5 |
| Cream | 7 |

## Vinyl Top Color Codes

| | |
|---|---|
| Ivory | 1 |
| Black | 2 |
| Cream | 7 |

## Options

| Sales Code | Description | Retail Price |
|---|---|---|
| | 2 dr hardtop coupe | $2,666.00 |
| | 2 dr convertible | 2,903.00 |

| Sales Code | Description | Retail Price |
|---|---|---|
| 341 | Manual rear antenna | |
| | (in lieu of front antenna) | 9.48 |
| 342 | Push-button radio w/manual antenna | 61.09 |
| 344 | Push-button AM/FM radio | |
| | w/manual antenna | 133.76 |
| 351 | Rear speaker | 15.80 |
| 354 | Delco stereo tape player | 128.49 |
| 361 | HD dual-stage air cleaner | 9.43 |
| 374 | Rear window defogger-blower | 21.06 |
| 382 | Door edge guards | NA |
| 391 | Visor vanity mirror | NA |
| 394 | Remote control OSRV mirror | NA |
| 401 | Luggage lamp | NA |
| 402 | Ignition switch lamp | NA |
| 421 | Underhood lamp | NA |
| 431 | Custom front & rear seatbelts | NA |
| 434 | Front shoulder belts | NA |
| 441 | Cruise control | 52.66 |
| 442 | Safeguard speedometer | NA |
| 444 | Rally gauges (& 702) | 31.60 |
| 452 | Wire wheel discs | 69.51 |
| 453 | Rally II wheels (available w/521) | |
| | Custom trim | 55.81 |
| | Std trim | 72.67 |
| 454 | Rally I wheels (available w/521) | |
| | Custom trim | 40.02 |
| | Std trim | 56.87 |
| 461 | Deluxe wheel discs | NA |
| 462 | Deluxe steering wheel | NA |
| 471 | Custom sports steering wheel | NA |
| 472 | Console (w/buckets & floor shift) | 47.39 |
| 474 | Electric clock | 15.80 |
| 481 | Dual exhaust (std w/HO, 400 engines) | 30.23 |
| 481 | Tailpipe extensions | NA |
| 491 | Rally stripes | NA |
| 494 | Dual horns (std w/custom trim) | NA |
| 501 | Power steering (17.5:1 ratio) | 94.79 |
| 502 | Power brakes w/pedal trim | 41.60 |
| 504 | Tilt steering wheel (NA w/std steering, | |
| | 3 speed column shift or Turbo | |
| | Hydra-matic wo/console) | NA |
| 514 | HD thermo fan | 15.80 |
| 521 | Front disc brakes | 63.19 |
| 524 | Custom shift knob | NA |
| 531 | Soft-Ray glass, all windows | 30.54 |
| 532 | Soft-Ray glass, windshield | 21.06 |
| 544 | Power convertible top | 52.66 |
| 551 | Power windows | 100.05 |
| 572 | Headrest (bench or bucket seat) | 52.66 |
| 582 | Custom AC | 355.98 |

| 621 | Ride & Handling Package | |
| | (std w/HO & 400 engines) | 9.32 |
| 631 | Front floor mats | NA |
| 632 | Rear floor mats | NA |
| 654 | Fold-down carpetback rear seat | 36.86 |
| 674 | HD alternator (std w/AC) | 15.80 |
| 678 | HD battery (incl w/674) | 3.48 |
| 681 | HD radiator (std w/AC) | 14.74 |
| 684 | HD fan (base, Sprint) | 8.43 |
| 704 | Hood tachometer | 63.19 |
| 731 | Safe-T-Track differential | NA |
| 738 | Rear axle options | NC |
| OBC | Custom trim option | 108.48 |
| OBC | Strato-Bench front seat | 31.60 |
| OBC-SVT | Vinyl roof | 84.26 |
| — | Stereo multiplex adapter | NA |
| — | Hood retainer pins | NA |
| — | Tu-tone | |
| | Std colors | 31.07 |
| | Custom colors | 114.27 |
| — | 185R–14 whitewall radial tires | |
| | 400 engine | 10.53 |
| | Others | 31.60 |
| — | E70–14 redline or whitewall tires | |
| | 400 engine | NC |
| | Others | 31.60 |

**Engines**

| L30 | 326 ci V–8 | 95.04 |
| L67 | 400 ci Ram Air | 263.30 |
| L76 | 326 ci HO V–8 | 169.70 |
| W53 | 230 ci Sprint ohc 6 cyl | 105.60 |
| W66 | 400 ci V–8 | |
| | W/TH400 transmission | 273.83 |
| | Wo/TH400 transmission | 358.09 |

## Facts

Although both the Camaro and the Firebird used the same body shell, chassis and suspension, the Firebird was a midyear introduction, released on February 23, 1967. The Camaro was introduced on September 26, 1966.

Two body styles were available: a two-door coupe and a two-door convertible. Five engines, combined with five models, were available.

The standard 230 ci six-cylinder was rated at 165 hp. Unlike other GM six-cylinder engines, the Pontiac six featured an overhead camshaft. Firebirds so equipped got 3.8 liter overhead cam lettering on both sides of the hood bulge.

An optional version of this engine, W53 rated at 215 hp, was offered on the Firebird Sprint models. It came with a hotter camshaft and a four-barrel Rochester Quadrajet carburetor. In addition to the hood bulge identification, Sprint models got ohc six emblems on the front part of the rocker panels. Bodyside tape stripes were optional.

The ohc six engine used the crankshaft and connecting rods from the Chevrolet six-cylinder engine.

The Firebird 326 models got a two-barrel version of Pontiac's 326 ci V-8, the L30 rated at 250 hp. The number 326 on the hood and trunk lid identified the Firebird as such. Firebird High Outputs (HOs) got the same engine, the L76, but with higher compression, a four-barrel Rochester Quadrajet carburetor and dual exhausts for a 285 hp output. The engine was officially known as the 326 HO. The corresponding Firebird model was the Firebird HO, which got unique HO side stripes for identification.

The biggest Firebird engine, the W66 displacing 400 ci, came with the 400 Firebird and was rated at 325 hp. The 400 came with a unique twin-scoop hood.

Transforming the 400 Firebird was the optional Ram Air Package. This made the 400's hood scoops functional and also changed the engine's designation to L67. Included was a hotter camshaft, stronger valvetrain and low-restriction cast-iron exhaust manifolds. Horsepower was unchanged at 325 but at a higher rpm, 5200, than with the regular 400. The 400 Ram Air also came with chrome valve covers, air cleaner and oil filler cap.

All 400 ci engines came with a throttle restrictor that stopped the carburetor's secondary barrels from opening all the way. This limited horsepower and allowed the Firebird to stay within the 10-lb-to-1-hp GM corporate edict.

Sixty-five Ram Air Firebirds were built in 1967—sixty-three hardtops and two convertibles. Both convertibles came with automatic transmissions.

All 1967 Firebirds came with manual steering, manual brakes and the monoleaf rear suspension. All models, except the base Firebirds, got traction bars on the right rear. Those equipped with the 326 HO and 400 ci V-8s got bars on both sides. The design of the bars used on the Firebirds differed from that of the bars used on the Camaro, and the bars were adustable. Optional were power steering, power brakes and power front disc brakes. Standard tires on all Firebirds were E70x14s.

The optional automatic on all models except those equipped with the 400 ci engines was the Powerglide two-speed automatic. All 400 ci cars got the three-speed Turbo Hydra-matic automatic.

Besides the various wheel covers, two styled steel wheels were available: the slotted Rally I and the five-spoke Rally II wheels.

The 1967 Firebirds were the only ones that came with side vent windows. The Firebird's VIN tag was located on the driver's-side door pillar. From 1968 on, as mandated by the federal government, all cars had their VIN tag mounted on the dash so that it would be easily visible through the windshield.

Optional was a fold-down rear seat on both body styles. Convertibles did not come with a power top—it was an option.

Total 326 HO production was 6,078 units; 400 production was 18,632.

*1967 Firebird 400*

# Chapter 2

# 1968 Firebird

## Production

| | |
|---|---|
| 2 dr coupe | 90,152 |
| 2 dr convertible | 16,960 |
| Total | 107,112 |

## Serial Numbers

**Description**
223378U100001
22337—model number (22337 = 2 dr coupe, 22367 = 2 dr convertible)
8—last digit of model year (8 = 1968)
U—assembly plant (U = Lordstown, L = Van Nuys)
100001—consecutive sequence number (100001 = 8 cyl, 600001 = 6 cyl)

**Location**
On plate attached to left side of dash, visible through windshield.

## Engine Identification Codes

ZK—250 ci I-6 1 bbl 175 hp manual
ZN—250 ci I-6 1 bbl 175 hp automatic
ZD—250 ci I-6 4 bbl 215 hp manual
ZE—250 ci I-6 4 bbl 215 hp automatic
WC—350 ci V-8 2 bbl 265 hp manual
YJ—350 ci V-8 2 bbl 265 hp automatic
WK—350 ci V-8 4 bbl 320 hp manual
YM—350 ci V-8 4 bbl 320 hp automatic
WZ—400 ci V-8 4 bbl 330 hp manual
YT—400 ci V-8 4 bbl 330 hp automatic
WQ—400 ci V-8 4 bbl 335 hp manual 400 HO
YW—400 ci V-8 4 bbl 335 hp automatic 400 HO
WI—400 ci V-8 4 bbl 335 hp manual Ram Air I
XN—400 ci V-8 4 bbl 335 hp automatic Ram Air I
WU—400 ci V-8 4 bbl 340 hp manual Ram Air II
XT—400 ci V-8 4 bbl 340 hp automatic Ram Air II

## Carburetors

350 ci 265 hp manual—7028071
350 ci 265 hp automatic—7028062
350 ci 320 hp manual—7028269
350 ci 320 hp automatic—7028266
400 ci 330 hp manual—7028265
400 ci 330 hp automatic—7028264

400 ci 335 hp manual HO—7028271
400 ci 335 hp automatic HO—7028264
400 ci 335 hp manual Ram Air I—7028277
400 ci 335 hp automatic Ram Air I—7028276
400 ci 340 hp manual Ram Air II—7028273
400 ci 340 hp automatic Ram Air II—7028270

## Distributors

350 ci 265 hp manual or
   automatic—1111281
350 ci 320 hp
   manual—1111447
350 ci 320 hp
   automatic—1111282
400 ci manual—1111449,
   1111448
400 ci automatic—1111270,
   1111300

## Head Castings

350 ci 265 hp—17
350 ci 320 hp—18
400 ci 330 hp—16;
   automatic—16/62
400 ci 335 hp HO—16
400 ci 335 hp Ram Air I—31
400 ci 340 hp Ram Air
   II—R(96)A

## Exterior Color Codes

| | | | |
|---|---|---|---|
| Starlight Black | A | Aleutian Blue | L |
| Cameo Ivory | C | Flambeau Burgundy | N |
| Alpine Blue | D | Springmist Green | P |
| Aegena Blue | E | Verdoro Green | Q |
| Nordic Blue | F | Solar Red | R |
| April Gold | G | Primavera Beige | T |
| Meridian Turquoise | K | Nightshade Green | V |
| | | Mayfair Maize | Y |

## Interior Trim Codes

| Color | Std Buckets | Custom Buckets | Bench | Custom Bench |
|---|---|---|---|---|
| Teal | 250 | 255 | — | — |
| Gold | 251 | 257 | — | — |
| Red | 252 | 258 | — | — |
| Black | 253 | 259 | 272 | 269 |
| Turquoise | 261 | 256 | — | — |
| Parchment | 262 | 260 | 273 | 275 |

## Convertible Top Color Codes

| | |
|---|---|
| White | 1 |
| Black | 2 |
| Teal | 5 |
| Gold | 8 |

## Vinyl Top Color Codes

| | |
|---|---|
| White | 1 |
| Black | 2 |
| Cream | 7 |

## Options

| Sales Code/ UPC | Description | Retail Price |
|---|---|---|
| | 2 dr hardtop coupe | $2,781.00 |
| | 2 dr convertible | 2,996.00 |

| Sales Code/ UPC | Description | Retail Price |
|---|---|---|
| 321 | Front foam cushion seats | 86.37 |
| 322 | Rear window defogger—Protection Group | 55.25 |
| 331 | Mirror Group (exc convertible) | 13.22 |
| 332 | Lamp Group | 5.25 |
| 342/W53 | Sprint ohc 6 cyl 4 bbl engine (wo/582) | 116.16 |
| 343/L30 | 350 ci V-8 2 bbl engine | 105.60 |
| 344/L76 | 350 ci HO V-8 4 bbl engine | 180.58 |
| 345/W66 | 400 ci V-8 4 bbl engine | |
| | W/351, 354, 358 | 273.83 |
| | Wo/351, 354, 358 | 358.09 |
| 347/L67 | 400 ci Ram Air V-8 4 bbl engine | |
| | (w/351, 354, 358; NA w/582) | 616.12 |
| 348/L74 | 400 ci HO V-8 4 bbl engine | |
| | (w/351, 354, 358) | 350.72 |
| 351 | Turbo Hydra-matic transmission | |
| | (w/345/W66, 347/L67, 348/L74) | 236.97 |
| 352 | Automatic transmission | |
| | (w/341, 342/W53, 343/L30, 344/L76) | 194.84 |
| 354 | 4 speed manual transmission w/floor shift | |
| | (wo/37S) | 184.31 |
| 355 | HD 3 speed manual transmission w/floor shift | |
| | W/343/L30, 344/L76 | 84.26 |
| | W/345/W66, 348/L74 | NC |
| 356 | HD 3 speed manual transmission w/floor shift | |
| | (w/472; incl w/342/W53) | 42.13 |
| 358 | Close-ratio 4 speed manual transmission | |
| | w/floor shift (required w/37S axle) | 184.31 |
| 361 | Safe-T-Track differential | |
| | Regular | 42.13 |
| | HD (w/H, K, P, S axles) | 63.19 |
| 381 | Manually operated rear antenna | 9.48 |
| 382 | Push-button radio & antenna | 61.09 |
| 384 | Push-button AM/FM radio & | |
| | manual antenna | 133.76 |
| 391 | Rear seat speaker | 15.80 |
| 394 | Stereo tape player (NA w/391, 392) | 133.76 |
| 402 | Spare tire cover | 5.27 |
| 404 | Rear window defogger (exc convertible) | 21.06 |
| 412 | Door edge guards | 6.24 |
| 414 | Dual horns | 4.21 |
| 421 | RH visor vanity mirror (exc w/422) | 2.11 |
| 422 | RH & LH visor vanity mirrors | 4.21 |
| 424 | LH remote control OSRV mirror | 9.48 |
| 431 | Custom front & rear seatbelts | 9.48 |
| 432 | Rear shoulder belts (w/431, 754) | 26.33 |
| 434 | Hood-mounted tachometer | 63.19 |
| 441 | Cruise control | 52.66 |
| 442 | Safeguard speedometer | 10.53 |
| 444 | Auxiliary gauge cluster | 31.60 |
| 452 | Wire wheel discs | 21.06 |

| | | |
|---|---|---:|
| 453 | Rally II rims | |
| | W/554 | 52.66 |
| | Wo/554 | 73.72 |
| 458 | Custom wheel discs | |
| | W/554 | 20.01 |
| | Wo/554 | 52.66 |
| 461 | Deluxe wheel discs | 21.06 |
| 462 | Deluxe steering wheel | 14.74 |
| 471 | Custom sport steering wheel | |
| | W/554 | 30.54 |
| | Wo/554 | 45.29 |
| 472 | Console (NA w/contour bench seat) | 50.55 |
| 474 | Electric clock (NA w/394) | 15.80 |
| 481 | Dual exhausts (w/343/L30) | 30.54 |
| 482 | Exhaust extensions | |
| | W/341, 342/W53, 343/L30 | 10.53 |
| | W/481, 344/L76, 345/W66, | |
| | 347/L67, 348/L74 | 21.06 |
| 492 | Remote control deck lid | 13.69 |
| 494 | Rally side stripes (NA w/344/L76) | 14.74 |
| 501 | Power steering | 69.51 |
| 502 | Power brakes | 42.13 |
| 504 | Tilt wheel (NA w/3 speed column shift or | |
| | Hydra-matic wo/console; | |
| | power steering required) | 42.13 |
| 514 | HD clutch & 7 blade fan (w/V-8, wo/582) | 15.80 |
| 521 | Front disc brakes | 63.19 |
| 524 | Custom gear shift knob (manual, floor shift) | 4.21 |
| 531 | Tinted glass, all windows | 30.54 |
| 532 | Tinted glass, windshield | 21.06 |
| 534 | Custom pedal trim (NA w/554) | 5.27 |
| 544 | Power convertible top | 52.66 |
| 551 | Power windows | 100.05 |
| 554 | Custom trim option | 114.88 |
| 561 | Full-width 4 way power bench seat | 69.51 |
| 564 | LH 4 way power bucket seat | 69.51 |
| 568 | Contour bench seat | 31.60 |
| 571 | Contoured head restraints | 52.66 |
| 582 | Custom AC | 360.20 |
| 591 | Speedometer gear adapter | 11.59 |
| 604 | Rear folding seat | 42.13 |
| 621 | Ride & Handling Package | |
| | W/345/W66 | 4.21 |
| | Wo/345/W66 | 9.48 |
| 631 | Front mats | 6.85 |
| 632 | Rear mats | 6.32 |
| 634 | Adjustable front & rear shock absorbers | 52.66 |
| 652 | Luggage lamp | 3.16 |
| 671 | Underhood lamp | 3.16 |
| 672 | Ignition switch lamp | 2.11 |
| 701 | HD battery (std w/4 bbl; 6 cyl wo/582) | 4.21 |
| 731 | HD air cleaner | 9.48 |

| Sales Code/ UPC | Description | Retail Price |
|---|---|---|
| 732 | Trunk mat | 8.43 |
| 754 | Front seat shoulder belts | |
| | W/431 | 26.33 |
| | Wo/431 | 23.17 |
| RTT | Two-tone paint (std color on coupe) | 31.60 |
| SPR | Special paint (code A only) | 10.53 |
| SPS | Special solid paint (exc code A) | 83.20 |
| STT | Special two-tone paint (coupe) | 114.80 |
| SVT | Cordova vinyl top (coupe) | 84.26 |
| THC | E70-14 red-stripe tires (w/341) | 31.60 |
| THD | E70-14 white-stripe tires (w/341) | 31.60 |
| THE | E70-14 blackwall tires (w/341) | NC |
| TKM | 195R-14 whitewall rayon radial tires (NA w/461) | |
| | W/341 | 56.87 |
| | W/342/W53, 343/L30, 344/L76 | 42.13 |
| | W/345/W66, 347/L67, 348/L74 | 10.53 |
| TMD | F70-14 whitewall nylon tires | |
| | W/341 | 46.34 |
| | W/342/W53, 343/L30, 344/L76 | 31.60 |
| | W/345/W66, 347/L67, 348/L74 | NC |
| TME | F70-14 blackwall nylon tires | |
| | W/341 | 14.74 |
| | W/342/W53, 343/L30, 344/L76 | NC |

## Facts

Visual changes were slight on the 1968 Firebirds, the most noticeable being the deletion of the side vent windows and the addition of rear side marker lights. With the deletion of the vent windows came Astro Ventilation. In the front, the turn signal lamps were redesigned to curve around the fender corners, thereby serving as front side marker lights as well.

Mechanically, the rear suspension was changed to a multileaf setup with staggered rear shock absorbers. The passenger's-side rear shock absorber was mounted behind the axle, and the driver's-side unit was mounted in front. Standard tire size was increased to F70x14—except on the base model, which got E70s. In January 1968, it was announced that Firebirds would get fiberglass-belted tires, an improvement over the usual bias-ply tires. Radial tires were optional.

The base Firebird still got the monoleaf rear springs.

The base engine, the ohc six, was stroked to give 250 ci with horsepower climbing to 175. The optional Sprint six retained the same 215 hp rating as in 1967 even with the increased displacement. With the increased displacement, the ohc six got a Pontiac crankshaft and rods.

The 326 ci V-8 was replaced by a 350 ci version rated at 265 hp. The 350 HO also got a corresponding horsepower increase to 320. All Pontiac V-8s came with redesigned cylinder heads that featured an open combustion chamber design and larger valves.

The W66 400 ci V-8 was uprated 5 hp to 330 hp. A new addition was the L74 400 HO, rated at 335 hp because of its stronger camshaft. The L67 400 Ram Air engine was still available, and it too was rated at 335 hp. As in 1967, the Ram Air engine came with the functional hood scoops.

On March 1, 1968, the Ram Air engine was deleted and replaced by the 400 Ram Air II engine, which still carried the L67 designation. Rated at 340 hp, the Ram Air II got revised cylinder heads that featured round exhaust ports, a forged crankshaft and pistons, and a higher-lift cam with a more durable valvetrain. Mandatory with the Ram Air II was either the four-speed manual or the Turbo Hydra-matic automatic. A total of 110 Firebirds were equipped with this engine—ninety-eight four-speeds and twelve automatics.

Although rated at 340 hp in the Firebird, the same engine was rated at 366 hp in the GTO. A throttle linkage restrictor stopped the rear two barrels of the Quadrajet from opening all the way, thus limiting horsepower and keeping the car within the 10-lb-to-1-hp corporate edict. All 400 ci engines were limited in this fashion.

Production of 400 Ram Airs was just 413— 321 four-speeds and ninety-two automatics. Production of 400 HOs amounted to 2,087.

Both Ram Air engines came with chrome valve covers, air cleaner and oil filler cap.

The 1968 Firebirds had their VIN tag located on the left side of the dash.

On March 4, 1968, the Van Nuys plant in Los Angeles began to assemble Firebirds.

*1968 Firebird 400*

# Chapter 3

# 1969 Firebird

## Production

| | |
|---|---|
| 2 dr coupe | 75,362 |
| 2 dr convertible | 11,649 |
| 2 dr coupe Trans Am | 689 |
| 2 dr convertible Trans Am | 8 |
| Total | 87,708 |

## Serial Numbers

### Description
223379N100001

22337—model number (22337 = 2 dr coupe, 22367 = 2 dr convertible)

9—last digit of model year (9 = 1969)

N—assembly plant (N = Norwood, L = Van Nuys, U = Lordstown)

100001—consecutive sequence number (100001 = 8 cyl, 600001 = 6 cyl)

### Location
On plate attached to left side of dash, visible through windshield.

## Engine Identification Codes
ZC—250 ci I-6 1 bbl 175 hp manual

ZF—250 ci I-6 1 bbl 175 hp automatic

ZH—250 ci I-6 1 bbl 230 hp manual

ZL—250 ci I-6 1 bbl 235 hp automatic

WC, WM—350 ci V-8 2 bbl 265 hp manual

XL, XB—350 ci V-8 2 bbl 265 hp automatic

YJ, YE—350 ci V-8 2 bbl 265 hp Powerglide w/AC, 3 speed manual wo/AC

WN—350 ci V-8 4 bbl 325 hp manual 350 HO

XC—350 ci V-8 4 bbl 325 hp automatic 350 HO

WZ—400 ci V-8 4 bbl 330 hp manual

YT—400 ci V-8 4 bbl 330 hp automatic

WQ—400 ci V-8 4 bbl 335 hp manual Ram Air III

YW—400 ci V-8 4 bbl 335 hp automatic Ram Air III

WH—400 ci V-8 4 bbl 345 hp manual Ram Air IV

XN—400 ci V-8 4 bbl 345 hp automatic Ram Air IV

## Carburetors
350 ci 265 hp manual—7028071

350 ci 265 hp automatic—7029062-72

350 ci 325 hp manual—7029263

350 ci 325 hp automatic—7029268
400 ci 330 hp manual—7029263
400 ci 330 hp automatic—7029268
400 ci 335 hp manual Ram Air III—7028273 or 7029273*
400 ci 335 hp automatic Ram Air III—7028270 or 7029270*
400 ci 345 hp manual Ram Air IV—7029273
400 ci 345 hp automatic Ram Air IV—7029270
*Late 1969.

## Distributors

350 ci 265 hp
  manual—1111960
350 ci 265 hp
  automatic—1111942
350 ci 325 hp
  manual—1111966
350 ci 325 hp
  automatic—1111965
400 ci manual—1111952
400 ci automatic—1111253,
  1111946
400 ci Ram Air—1111941

## Head Castings

350 ci 265 hp—47
350 ci 325 hp—48
400 ci 330 hp—16;
  automatic—16, 62 w/AC
400 ci 335 hp Ram Air III—48;
  automatic—16, 62 w/AC
400 ci 345 hp Ram Air IV—722

## Exterior Color Codes

| | | | |
|---|---|---|---|
| Cameo White | C | Burgundy | N |
| Warwick Blue | D | Palladium Silver | P |
| Liberty Blue | E | Verdoro Green | Q |
| Windward Blue | F | Matador Red | R |
| Antique Gold | G | Champagne | S |
| Limelight Green | H | Carousel Red | T |
| Crystal Turquoise | K | Goldenrod Yellow | W |
| Midnight Green | M | | |

## Interior Trim Codes

| Color | Std Buckets | Custom Buckets | Bench |
|---|---|---|---|
| Blue | 200 | 210 | — |
| Gold | 202 | 212 | — |
| Red | — | 214 | — |
| Green | 206 | 216 | — |
| Parchment | 207 | 217 | 227 |
| Black | 208 | 218 | 228 |
| Gold Leather | — | 293 | — |

## Convertible Top Color Codes

| | |
|---|---|
| White | 1 |
| Black | 2 |
| Blue | 3 |
| Green | 9 |

## Vinyl Top Color Codes

| | |
|---|---|
| Black | 2 |
| Blue | 3 |
| Parchment | 5 |
| Fawn | 8 |
| Green | 9 |

# Options

| Sales Code/UPC | Description | Retail Price |
|---|---|---|
| | 2 dr coupe | $2,821.00 |
| | 2 dr convertible | 3,045.00 |
| 321/Y88 | Basic Group | 113.75 |
| 322/WS4 | Trans Am option (w/354/M20 only) | 724.60 |
| 324/Y86 | Decor Group | 62.14 |
| 331/WS6 | Power Assist Group | |
| | W/341/std, 342/W53 | 364.93 |
| | W/343/L30 | 375.49 |
| | W/344/L76, 345/W66, 347/L67, 348/L74 | 396.61 |
| 332/WS5 | Turnpike Cruise Group (w/Hydra-matic, V-8, 501/N41) | 176.94 |
| 334/WS8 | Rally Group | |
| | All 345/W66, 347/L67, 348/L74 w/324/Y86 | 149.55 |
| | All 345/W66, 347/L67, 348/L74 wo/324/Y86 | 186.41 |
| | All 341/std, 342/W53, 343/L30, 344/L76 w/324/Y86 | 154.82 |
| | All 341/std, 342/W53, 343/L30, 344/L76 wo/324/Y86 | 191.68 |
| 341/Std | Ohc 6 cyl 1 bbl engine | NC |
| 342/W53 | Sprint sport option (wo/582/C60) | 129.54 |
| 343/L30 | Firebird 350 sport option | 110.59 |
| 344/L76 | Firebird HO sport option | 199.05 |
| 345/W66 | Firebird 400 sport option | |
| | Coupe w/351/M40, 354/M20, 358/M21 | 347.56 |
| | Convertible w/351/M40, 354/M20, 358/M21 | 331.76 |
| | Coupe wo/351/M40, 354/M20, 358/M21 | 431.81 |
| | Convertible wo/351/M40, 354/M20, 358/M21 | 416.01 |
| 347/L67 | 400 ci Ram Air IV V-8 4 bbl engine (w/345/W66) | 558.20 |
| 348/L74 | 400 ci Ram Air V-8 4 bbl engine (w/345/W66) | 76.88 |
| 351/M40 | Turbo Hydra-matic (w/344/L76, 345/W66, 347/L67, 348/L74) | 227.04 |
| 352/M31 | 2 speed automatic transmission | |
| | W/341/std | 163.68 |
| | W/343/L30 | 174.24 |
| 353/Std | 3 speed manual transmission w/column shift (w/341/std, 343/L30, 344/L76) | NC |
| 354/M20 | 4 speed manual transmission w/floor shift (w/all exc 347/L67, V-8 engine; w/3.90, 4.33 axles) | 195.36 |

| | | |
|---|---|---|
| 355/M13 | HD 3 speed manual transmission | |
| | w/floor shift (w/343/L30, 344/L76) | 84.26 |
| 356/M12 | 3 speed manual transmission w/floor shift | |
| | W/341/std | 42.13 |
| | W/342/W53 | NC |
| 358/M21 | Close-ratio 4 speed manual transmission | |
| | w/floor shift (w/390) | 195.36 |
| 359/M38 | Turbo Hydra-matic transmission | |
| | W/341/std, 342/W53 | 195.36 |
| | W/343/L30 | 205.92 |
| 361/G80 | Safe-T-Track axle | |
| | Regular | 42.13 |
| | HD | 63.19 |
| 362/G94–G83 | Special order axle | 2.11 |
| 364/G95–G97 | Economy axle | 2.11 |
| 368/G90–G92 | Performance axle | 2.11 |
| 382/U63 | AM radio w/manual antenna | 61.09 |
| 384/U69 | AM/FM radio w/manual antenna | 133.76 |
| 388/U58 | AM/FM stereo radio w/manual antenna | 239.08 |
| 391/U80 | Rear speaker (NA w/388/U58, 394/U57) | 15.80 |
| 394/U57 | Stereo tape player (NA w/391/U80) | 133.76 |
| 402/P17 | Spare tire cover (NA w/708/N65) | 5.27 |
| 404/C50 | Rear window defogger | |
| | (NA w/convertible) | 22.12 |
| 412/B93 | Door edge guards | 6.24 |
| 414/U05 | Dual horns | 4.21 |
| 421/D34 | RH visor vanity mirror | 2.11 |
| 422/DH5 | LH visor vanity mirror | 2.11 |
| 424/D33 | Remote control OSRV mirror | 10.53 |
| 431/WS1 | Custom front seatbelts & shoulder straps | |
| | Coupe | 12.64 |
| | Convertible | 36.86 |
| 432/WS2 | Custom seatbelts & | |
| | front & rear shoulder straps | |
| | Coupe | 38.97 |
| | Convertible | 63.19 |
| 438/AS1 | Front shoulder straps (convertible only) | 10.53 |
| 441/K30 | Cruise control (w/automatic, V-8 only) | 57.93 |
| 442/U15 | Safeguard speedometer | |
| | (NA w/484/W63, 444/U30) | 11.59 |
| 444/U30 | Rally gauge cluster & tachometer | |
| | (wo/442/U15, 474/U35, 484/W63) | 84.26 |
| 451/P01 | Deluxe wheel cover | 21.06 |
| 452/P02 | Custom wheel covers | |
| | W/324/Y86 | 20.01 |
| | Wo/324/Y86 | 41.07 |
| 453/N95 | Wire wheel covers | |
| | W/324/Y86 | 52.66 |
| | Wo/324/Y86 | 73.72 |
| 454/N98 | Rally II wheels | |
| | W/324/Y86 | 63.19 |
| | Wo/324/Y86 | 84.26 |

| Sales Code/UPC | Description | Retail Price |
|---|---|---|
| 461/N30 | Deluxe steering wheel | 15.80 |
| 462/N34 | Custom sports steering wheel | |
| | W/324/Y86 | 34.76 |
| | Wo/324/Y86 | 50.55 |
| 471/UB5 | Hood-mounted tachometer | 63.19 |
| 472/D55 | Console (w/bucket seats) | 53.71 |
| 474/U35 | Electric clock | |
| | (incl w/484/W63; NA w/444/U30) | 15.80 |
| 481/N10 | Dual exhausts (available w/343/L30) | 30.54 |
| 484/W63 | Rally gauge cluster w/clock | |
| | (wo/442/U15, 444/U30) | 47.39 |
| 492/A90 | Remote control deck lid release | 14.74 |
| 501/N41 | Variable-ratio power steering | 105.32 |
| 502/J50 | Power brakes (NA w/345/W66, | |
| | 347/L67, 348/L74) | 42.13 |
| 504/N33 | Tilt steering (NA w/std steering or | |
| | column shift manual transmission) | 45.29 |
| 511/JL2 | Power front disc brakes | 64.25 |
| 514/JL1 | Custom pedal trim plates | 5.27 |
| 531/A01 | Tinted glass, all windows | 32.65 |
| 532/A02 | Tinted glass, windshield | 22.12 |
| 534/M09 | Gear knob (floor shift, | |
| | manual transmission) | 5.27 |
| 544/C06 | Power convertible top | 52.66 |
| 551/A31 | Power windows | 105.32 |
| 554/W54 | Custom trim option | |
| | W/knit-vinyl bench seat (coupe) | 110.99 |
| | W/bucket seats | 78.99 |
| | W/leather bucket seats | 199.05 |
| 564/A46 | LH power bucket seat | 73.72 |
| 582/C60 | Custom AC (NA w/Sprint or Ram Air) | 375.99 |
| 588/C57 | Power flow ventilation (NA w/582/C60) | 42.13 |
| 604/A67 | Rear folding seat | 42.13 |
| 621/Y96 | Ride & Handling springs & shocks | |
| | W/345/W66, 347/L67, 348/L74 | 4.21 |
| | W/341/std, 342/W53, 343/L30, 344/L76 | 9.48 |
| 631/B32 | Front floor mats | 6.85 |
| 632/B33 | Rear floor mats | 6.32 |
| 652/U25 | Luggage lamp | 3.16 |
| 671/U26 | Underhood lamp | 4.21 |
| 672/UA1 | HD battery (std w/344/L76, 345/W66, | |
| | 347/L67, 348/L74, 582/C60) | 4.21 |
| 682/K82 | HD 55 amp alternator | |
| | (w/341/std, 342/W53) | 15.80 |
| 688/K96 | 55 amp alternator (V-8 only; | |
| | NA w/582/C60; w/343/L30, 344/L76) | 26.33 |
| 691/K02 | HD fan w/fan clutch (NA w/341/std, | |
| | 347/L67, 348/L74, 582/C60) | 15.80 |
| 692/KB2 | HD Power-Flex fan | |
| | All wo/582/C60 | 10.53 |
| | V-8 w/582/C60 | NC |

| Sales Code/UPC | Description | Retail Price |
|---|---|---|
| 694/V64 | Instant-Aire pump (NA w/347/L67, 611) | 15.80 |
| 701/V01 | HD radiator (NA w/582/C60) | 14.74 |
| 708/N65 | Space-Saver spare tire | |
| | Wo/454/N98 | 15.80 |
| | W/454/N98 | NC |
| 731/K45 | HD dual-stage air cleaner | 9.48 |
| GF/PX5 | F78-14 black tire | 14.74 |
| GR/PX6 | F78-14 whitewall tire | 28.44 |
| HR/PL3 | E78-14 white tire (w/341/std) | 26.33 |
| MT/PY4 | F70-14 whitewall tire | 74.78 |
| MT/PY5 | F70-14 redwall tire | 74.78 |
| RTT/— | Std two-tone color (exc convertible) | 31.60 |
| SPO/— | Special solid colors | |
| | Coupe wo/vinyl top | 115.85 |
| | Coupe or convertible w/vinyl top | 100.05 |
| SPR/— | Special color codes F, T, W | 12.64 |
| STT/— | Special two-tone color (exc convertible) | 147.45 |
| SVT/G08 | Cordova top (coupe) | 89.52 |

## Facts

Although considered first-generation Firebirds, the 1969 models received an extensive exterior facelift along with a new interior. Still available as a coupe and a convertible, their most noticeable change was the new one-piece Lexan front bumper-grille. The car was still built on the 108 in. wheelbase, but it was longer, wider and heavier.

All Firebirds got a steering column ignition and steering gearshift interlock designed to deter theft. The ignition key receptacle was also located on the steering column. The optional power steering unit included a variable ratio, and the optional disc brakes featured a new single piston caliper.

Engine specs for the 250 ci ohc six and the 350 ci two-barrel V-8 were unchanged from those in 1968. The L76 350 HO was uprated to 325 hp thanks to a different cam and new cylinder heads.

The regular 400 and the 400 HO—also known as the Ram Air III—were basically carryovers from 1968.

Under the L67 designation was the 400 Ram Air IV, which pumped out 345 hp. Differing from the previous Ram Air II, it had an aluminum intake manifold, 1.65:1 ratio rocker arms and oblong combustion chambers for better flow. It also had the four-bolt main block—as did the 400 HO.

Identification between the differing Firebird models was similar to that between previous offerings. The base six-cylinder Firebird got Overhead Cam 4.1 liter lettering on both sides of the hood bulge. The optional Sprint six got additional rocker panel emblems. The 350 ci powered cars got 350 emblems on both sides of the hood bulge, but the only way you could identify 350 HO powered Firebirds was by the air cleaner decal, as the HO side stripes were deleted in 1969.

The 400 powered Firebirds came with the twin hood scoops and 400 hood and trunk lid emblems.

The 1969 Firebirds were also built at an additional location: the Norwood, Ohio, plant.

Three types of Ram Air hoods were offered. The first design, which was introduced as a mid 1968 modification, let the driver control the intake of outside air by means of cable-operated flapper valves. This was standard with the L67 Ram Air IV and optional with the L74 400 ci V-8s. The second system included underhood-grille-mounted air intakes to complement the hood-mounted system. The Trans Am got the third hood with forward-mounted scoops.

Discontinued during the model year were the optional adjustable Koni shocks and the optional wire wheel covers.

Headrests were optional at the beginning of the model year but became standard equipment by midyear.

In March, the Firebird Trans Am became available. In its first year of production, the Trans Am was an option package, WS4, available on the coupe or convertible. It consisted of the 400 HO engine, three-speed manual transmission, heavy-duty suspension with front and rear sway bars, power steering and brakes, and Safe-T-Track rear. Visually, the Trans Am could be identified by functional front fender air extractors, dual hood-roof-deck stripes, a hood that had wider scoops located just behind the bumper, a blacked-out grille and a rear deck spoiler. In the interior, the Trans Am got a three-spoke wood-grain steering wheel. Optional was the 400 Ram Air IV engine, with a four-speed manual or Turbo Hydramatic automatic transmission. Trans Am decals were located on the front fenders. The Trans Am was available in only one color, Cameo White.

A total of 689 Trans Am coupes were built—634 with the 400 HO engine, broken down as 114 with a manual transmission and 520 with the automatic. Ram Air IV powered Trans Ams were produced as follows: forty-six with a manual and nine with the automatic. The eight convertibles built were all powered by the 400 HO and were split evenly between manual and automatic transmissions.

*1969 Firebird 400*

# Chapter 4

# 1970 Firebird

## Production

| Model | Manual | Automatic | Total |
|---|---|---|---|
| 2 dr base 6 cyl | | | 3,134 |
| 2 dr base 8 cyl | 2,899* | 15,975* | 15,740 |
| 2 dr Esprit 8 cyl | 2,104 | 16,857 | 18,961 |
| 2 dr Formula 400 8 cyl | 2,777 | 4,931 | 7,708 |
| 2 dr Trans Am Ram Air III 8 cyl | 1,769 | 1,339 | 3,108 |
| 2 dr Trans Am Ram Air IV 8 cyl | 29 | 59 | 88 |
| Total | 9,578 | 39,161 | 48,739 |

*Includes six- and eight-cylinders.

## Serial Numbers

**Description**
223870L100001
22387—model number (22387 = base, 22487 = Esprit,
   22687 = Formula 400, 22887 = Trans Am)
0—last digit of model year (0 = 1970)
L—assembly plant (L = Van Nuys, N = Norwood)
100001—consecutive sequence number (100001 = 8 cyl, 600001 =
   6 cyl)

**Location**
   On plate attached to left side of dash, visible through
windshield.

## Engine Identification Codes
ZB—250 ci I-6 1 bbl 155 hp manual
ZG—250 ci I-6 1 bbl 155 hp automatic
WU—350 ci V-8 2 bbl 255 hp manual
YU—350 ci V-8 2 bbl 255 hp automatic
XX—400 ci V-8 2 bbl 265 hp automatic
WT—400 ci V-8 2 bbl 330 hp manual
YS—400 ci V-8 2 bbl 330 hp automatic
WS—400 ci V-8 2 bbl 345 hp manual Ram Air III
YZ—400 ci V-8 2 bbl 345 hp automatic Ram Air III
WW—400 ci V-8 2 bbl 370 hp manual Ram Air IV
XP—400 ci V-8 2 bbl 370 hp automatic Ram Air IV

## Carburetors
350 ci 255 hp manual—7040071, 7040471
350 ci 255 hp automatic—7040062, 7040063 w/AC

400 ci 265 hp automatic—7040060, 7040061, 7040062
400 ci 330 hp manual—7040263, 7040563
400 ci 330 hp automatic—7040273, 7040573
400 ci 335 hp manual Ram Air III—7040273, 7040573 Calif
400 ci 335 hp automatic Ram Air III—7040270, 7040570 Calif
400 ci 345 hp manual Ram Air IV—7040273, 7040573 Calif
400 ci 345 hp automatic Ram Air IV—7040270, 7040570 Calif

## Distributors
350 ci—1112008
400 ci 265 hp—1112007
400 ci manual—1111176
400 ci manual Ram Air
  III—1112010
400 ci automatic—1111148
400 ci automatic Ram Air
  III—1112009
400 ci Ram Air IV—1112011

## Head Castings
350 ci 255 hp—11
400 ci 265 hp—11
400 ci 330 hp—12;
  automatic—13
400 ci 345 hp Ram Air III—12;
  automatic—12, 13
400 ci 370 hp Ram Air IV—614

## Exterior Color Codes

| | | | |
|---|---|---|---|
| Polar White | 10 | Goldenrod Yellow | 51 |
| Palladium Silver | 14 | Coronado Gold | 53 |
| Bermuda Blue | 25 | Granada Gold | 58 |
| Lucerne Blue | 26 | Palomino Copper | 63 |
| Keylime Green | 43 | Carousel Red | 65 |
| Palisade Green | 45 | Castillian Bronze | 67 |
| Verdoro Green | 47 | Cardinal Red | 75 |

## Interior Trim Codes

| Color | Std Buckets | Custom Buckets |
|---|---|---|
| Blue | 201 | 211 |
| Red | — | 214 |
| Saddle | 205 | 215 |
| Green | 206 | 216 |
| Sandalwood | 207 | 217/217* |
| Black | 208 | 218/228* |
| *Cloth/vinyl. | | |

## Vinyl Top Color Codes

| | | | | |
|---|---|---|---|---|
| Black | 2 | Fawn | | 8 |
| Blue | 3 | Green | | 9 |
| Parchment | 5 | | | |

## Options

| Sales Code | Description | Retail Price |
|---|---|---|
| | 2 dr coupe | $2,875.00 |
| | 2 dr Formula 400 | 3,370.00 |
| | 2 dr Trans Am | 4,305.00 |
| | 2 dr Esprit | 3,241.00 |
| 321 | Basic Group (all exc 22887) | 103.22 |

| 331 | Power Assist Group | |
|------|-------------------|-----:|
| | 22387 w/341 | 342.81 |
| | 22387, 22487 w/343 | 353.37 |
| | 22487 w/346; 22687 | 374.49 |
| 343 | 350 ci V-8 2V engine (std w/22487; | |
| | NA w/351, 358) | 110.59 |
| 346 | 400 ci V-8 2V engine | |
| | (22487 w/350) | 52.66 |
| 348 | 400 ci Ram Air V-8 4V engine | |
| | (std w/Trans Am; NA w/352, 359, 754) | 168.51 |
| 351 | Turbo Hydra-matic transmission | |
| | 22487, 22687; NA w/341, 343 | 227.04 |
| | 22887 | NC |
| 352 | 2 speed automatic transmission | |
| | 22387 w/341 | 163.68 |
| | 22387, 22487 w/343 | 174.24 |
| 354 | 4 speed manual transmission | |
| | w/floor shift (requires V-8; | |
| | NA w/754) | 195.36 |
| 355 | HD 3 speed manual transmission | |
| | w/floor shift (wo/341; std w/22687) | 84.26 |
| 358 | Close-ratio 4 speed manual transmission | |
| | w/floor shift (22687 w/37R axle; | |
| | 22887 w/37R axle; NC required w/361) | 195.36 |
| 359 | Turbo Hydra-matic transmission | |
| | 22387, 22487 w/343 | 205.92 |
| | 22387 w/341 | 195.36 |
| 361 | Safe-T-Track differential | |
| | (std w/Trans Am; requires 37R axle) | 42.13 |
| 368 | Performance axle | 10.53 |
| 401 | Push-button AM radio | 61.09 |
| 402 | Push-button AM/FM radio | 133.76 |
| 402 | Spare tire cover | 5.27 |
| 404 | AM/FM stereo radio | 239.08 |
| 411 | Rear speaker | 15.80 |
| 412 | Stereo tape player (regular w/radio; | |
| | NA w/411) | 133.76 |
| 431 | Decor moldings (22387, 22687 only; | |
| | std on others) | 47.49 |
| 432 | Recessed windshield wipers | |
| | 22387, 22687; std w/others) | 18.96 |
| 434 | Dual body-color sport-type | |
| | OSRV mirrors (22387) | 26.33 |
| 441 | LH visor vanity mirror | 2.11 |
| 451 | Custom front & rear seatbelts & | |
| | front shoulder straps | 12.64 |
| 452 | Custom front & rear seatbelts & | |
| | shoulder straps | 38.97 |
| 461 | Deluxe steering wheel (22387; | |
| | std w/22487, 22687) | 15.80 |

| Sales Code | Description | Retail Price |
|---|---|---|
| 464 | Formula steering wheel (w/501 only) | |
| | In 22487; 22687 | 42.13 |
| | In 22387; NC in 22887 | 57.93 |
| 471 | Wheel trim rings (22387, 22687 wo/464; | |
| | std w/22487) | 21.06 |
| 473 | Wire wheel discs | |
| | 22487 | 52.66 |
| | 22387, 22687 | 73.72 |
| 474 | Rally II rims | |
| | 22487 | 63.19 |
| | 22387, 22687 (incl 471; std w/22887) | 84.26 |
| 481 | Cruise control | 57.93 |
| 484 | Rally cluster w/clock (std w/Trans Am; | |
| | NA w/341, 484, 652) | 94.79 |
| 488 | Rally cluster w/clock (exc Trans Am; | |
| | NA w/341, 484, 652) | 47.39 |
| 492 | Electric clock (exc Trans Am; NA w/652) | 15.80 |
| 494 | Front console (NA in 6 cyl | |
| | w/3 speed transmission) | 58.98 |
| 501 | Variable-ratio power steering | |
| | (std w/22887) | 105.32 |
| 502 | Wonder Touch power brakes | |
| | (std w/22887) | 42.13 |
| 504 | Tilt steering wheel (regular w/501; | |
| | NA w/column shift) | 45.29 |
| 521 | 1 pair front floor mats | 6.85 |
| 522 | 1 pair rear floor mats | 6.32 |
| 524 | Fitted trunk floor mats (std w/22487; | |
| | incl w/731) | 8.43 |
| 531 | Soft-Ray tinted glass, all windows | 32.65 |
| 532 | Soft-Ray tinted glass, windshield only | 26.33 |
| 534 | Electric rear window defroster | |
| | (V-8 only) | 52.66 |
| 541 | Rear window defogger | 26.33 |
| 551 | Power side windows (all w/494) | 105.32 |
| 552 | Power door locks & seatback locks | |
| | (NA w/734) | 68.46 |
| 554 | Remote control deck lid release | 14.74 |
| 582 | Custom AC | 375.99 |
| 591 | Speedometer gear adapter | 11.59 |
| 634 | Rear lamp monitor | 26.33 |
| 652 | Warning lamp (exc 22887; | |
| | NA w/484 or 488) | 36.86 |
| 661 | Convenience lamps | 11.59 |
| 674 | Dual horns (22387; std in others) | 4.21 |
| 684 | Door edge guards | 6.32 |
| 692 | HD battery | 4.21 |
| 704 | Space-Saver spare tire | |
| | Exc 22887; std w/474 or TNL | 15.80 |
| | 22887 | NC |

| | | |
|---|---|---:|
| 711 | Evaporative emission control | |
| | (required in Calif cars) | 36.86 |
| 731 | Custom Trim Group (std 22487) | 77.94 |
| 731 | HD air cleaner (exc Trans Am; NA w/348) | 9.48 |
| 734 | Power door locks only | 45.29 |
| 741 | Roof dip moldings (std w/22487) | 31.60 |
| 754 | Mountain performance axles | |
| | 22387, 22487 wo/582 | 16.85 |
| | 343 w/352, 359; 22387, 22487 w/582 | 2.11 |
| SVT | Cordova vinyl top | |
| | 22387, 22687 wo/431 | 89.52 |
| | 22387, 22687 w/431 & 22487 | 73.72 |
| TGR | F78-14 whitewall tires | |
| | (22387, 22487 w/341, 343, 346) | 43.18 |
| THR | E78-14 whitewall tires | |
| | (22387, 22487 w/341, 343, 346) | 26.33 |
| TMF | F70-14 blackwall tires | |
| | (22387, 22487 w/341, 343, 346) | 35.81 |
| TML | F70-14 raised-letter tires | |
| | 22387, 22487 w/341, 343, 346 | 64.25 |
| | 22687 | 28.44 |
| TNL | F60-15 raised-letter tires | |
| | (22687; incl 15 in. Rally II wheels) | 146.39 |

## Facts

The 1970 Firebird was totally redesigned—it was longer, lower and heavier with just one body style, a semifastback hardtop. Until 1982, Firebirds would be available in this basic body in four models: the base Firebird, the luxury Esprit, the Formula and the Trans Am.

Because the Firebird models were introduced at the Chicago Auto Show on February 26, 1970, they would normally have been thought of as 1970½s; however all were in fact 1970 models.

The base Firebird got a front stabilizer bar and manual disc brakes as standard equipment. The base engine was the Chevrolet inline six, as the Pontiac ohc six was dropped. Optional on the base model was the two-barrel version of the 350 ci V-8.

The Esprit came with the 350 ci V-8 two-barrel, manual disc brakes and a three-speed manual transmission with a floor-mounted shifter. The only optional engine on the Esprit was the two-barrel version of the 400 ci V-8 rated at 265 hp. The custom interior was standard on the Esprit model, as were dual body-color rearview mirrors, exterior moldings, trim rings, concealed windshield wipers and other trim items.

The Formula 400 got a firmer suspension with a rear sway bar and the L78 400 ci V-8 rated at 330 hp mated to a three-speed manual transmission. Optional was the L74 400 Ram Air III engine. With the Ram Air III, the Formula 400's unique twin-scoop fiberglass hood got functional scoops. Formula 400 emblems were located on the front fenders beneath the regular Firebird script. Ram Air cars also got Ram Air decals on the hood scoops.

The top-performance Firebird was the Trans Am. It came with a front air dam, a rear spoiler, rear wheel air deflectors, front fender air extractors and a rear-facing functional hood scoop. Fifteen-inch Rally II wheels, without trim rings, with F60x15 raised white-letter tires were used. Other exterior features were concealed wipers and dual body-color rearview mirrors. Trans Ams were available in Cameo White with a blue-black stripe or Lucerne Blue with a black-bordered white stripe. On the Endura bumper, a Firebird decal was used. Trans Am decals were located on the front fenders behind the wheelwells.

In the black or red Trans Am interior, engine-turned aluminum inserts were used on the dash panel; all other Firebirds got a wood-grain effect. The Trans Am included the functional U30 Rally gauges: tachometer, clock, voltmeter, oil pressure, water temperature and fuel. Seats were a low-back-cum-headrest design. Trans Ams also got the Formula three-spoke urethane-rimmed steering wheel.

Standard engine on the Trans Am was the L74 Ram Air III rated at 335 hp. Optional was the LS1 400 ci 345 hp V-8. Both

*1970 Firebird Trans Am*

engines got chrome engine dress-up, dual exhausts with chrome outlets and the M20 wide-ratio transmission as standard equipment. Optional transmissions were the M21 close-ratio box and the Turbo Hydra-matic automatic.

Suspensions on the Trans Am included heavy-duty springs, shocks, and 1.25 in. front and 0.875 in. rear sway bars. Power front disc brakes were standard, as was variable-ratio power steering. The Safe-T-Track limited-slip rear was also standard.

All 1970 four-speed manual transmissions and the Formula's standard three-speed manual came with Hurst shifters.

The two-speed Powerglide was still in production, available with the six-cylinder or 350 ci V-8 engines only.

The custom interior was optional on the Formula and Trans Am.

The grille had a tight, square mesh.

Firebirds equipped with a radio got in-glass windshield antennas.

# Chapter 5

# 1971 Firebird

## Production

| Model | Manual | Automatic | Total |
|---|---|---|---|
| 2 dr base 6 cyl | | | 2,975 |
| 2 dr base 8 cyl | 2,778* | 20,244* | 20,047 |
| 2 dr Esprit 8 cyl | 947 | 19,238 | 20,185 |
| 2 dr Formula 400 8 cyl | 1,860 | 5,942 | 7,802 |
| 2 dr Trans Am 8 cyl | 885 | 1,231 | 2,116 |
| Total | 6,470 | 46,655 | 53,125 |

*Includes six- and eight-cylinders.

## Serial Numbers

**Description**
223871L100001
22387—model number (22387 = base, 22487 = Esprit, 22687 = Formula 400, 22887 = Trans Am)
1—last digit of model year (1 = 1971)
L—assembly plant (L = Van Nuys, N = Norwood)
100001—consecutive sequence number (100001 = 8 cyl, 600001 = 6 cyl)

**Location**
On plate attached to left side of dash, visible through windshield.

## Engine Identification Codes
ZB, CAA—250 ci I-6 1 bbl 155 hp manual (110 hp net)
ZG, CAB—250 ci I-6 1 bbl 155 hp automatic
WR—350 ci V-8 2 bbl 250 hp 3 speed manual (165 hp net)
WU—350 ci V-8 2 bbl 250 hp 4 speed manual
YU—350 ci V-8 2 bbl 250 hp Powerglide automatic
XR—350 ci V-8 2 bbl 250 hp Turbo Hydra-matic automatic
XX—400 ci V-8 2 bbl 265 hp automatic (180 hp net)
WT—400 ci V-8 4 bbl 300 hp 3 speed manual (250 hp net)
WK—400 ci V-8 4 bbl 300 hp 4 speed manual
YS—400 ci V-8 4 bbl 300 hp automatic
YC—455 ci V-8 4 bbl 325 hp automatic (255 hp net)
WL—455 ci V-8 4 bbl 335 hp 3 speed manual (305 hp net)
WC—455 ci V-8 4 bbl 335 hp 4 speed manual
YE—455 ci V-8 4 bbl 335 hp automatic

## Carburetors
350 ci 250 hp manual—7041171
350 ci 250 hp automatic—7041162, 7041163 or 7041172 w/AC

400 ci 265 hp automatic—7041160, 7041161 or 7041170 w/AC
400 ci 300 hp manual—7041263
400 ci 300 hp automatic—7041264, 7041271
455 ci 325 hp automatic—7041262, 7041271
455 ci 335 hp manual—7041267, 7041273
455 ci 335 hp automatic—7041268, 7041270

## Head Castings

| | | | |
|---|---|---|---|
| 350 ci 250 hp—94 | | 455 ci 325 hp—66 | |
| 400 ci 265 hp—99 | | 455 ci 335 hp—197 | |
| 400 ci 300 hp—96 | | | |

## Exterior Color Codes

| | | | |
|---|---|---|---|
| Cameo White | 11 | Quezal Gold | 53 |
| Nordic Silver | 13 | Aztec Gold | 59 |
| Starlight Black | 19 | Sandalwood | 61 |
| Adriatic Blue | 24 | Canyon Copper | 62 |
| Lucerne Blue | 26 | Castillian Bronze | 67 |
| Limekist Green | 42 | Cardinal Red | 75 |
| Laurentian Green | 49 | Rosewood | 78 |
| Tropical Lime | 52 | | |

## Interior Trim Codes

| Color | Std Buckets | Custom Buckets |
|---|---|---|
| Blue | 201 | 211 |
| Ivory | — | 212 |
| Saddle | 203 | 213 |
| Sienna | — | 214 |
| Jade | 206 | 216 |
| Sandalwood | 207 | 217/227* |
| Black | 209 | 219/229* |

*Cloth/vinyl.

## Vinyl Top Color Codes

| | |
|---|---|
| Black | Dark Brown |
| White | Dark Green |
| Sandalwood | |

## Options

| Sales Code/UPC | Description | Retail Price |
|---|---|---|
| | 2 dr coupe | $3,047.00 |
| | 2 dr coupe Esprit | 3,416.00 |
| | 2 dr coupe Formula 400 | 3,445.00 |
| | 2 dr coupe Trans Am | 4,595.00 |
| 34D/L30 | 350 ci V-8 2V engine (22387) | 121.12 |
| 34G/L65 | 400 ci V-8 2V engine (22487) | 52.66 |
| 34L/L78 | 400 ci V-8 4V engine (22687) | 100.05 |
| 34P/L75 | 455 ci V-8 4V engine (22687 only) | 157.98 |
| 34U/LS5 | 455 ci HO V-8 4V engine (22687 only; std w/22887) | 236.97 |

| Sales Code/UPC | Description | Retail Price |
|---|---|---|
| 35A/Std | 3 speed manual transmission w/column shift (22387 6 cyl only) | NC |
| 35B/M12 | 3 speed manual transmission w/floor shift (w/34A, 34D/L30) | 10.53 |
| 35C/M13 | HD 3 speed manual transmission w/floor shift (NA w/34A, 34G/L65) | 84.26 |
| 35F/M20 | 4 speed manual transmission (NA w/34A, 22887) | 205.97 |
| 35G/M22 | Close-ratio 4 speed manual transmission (NA w/34A, 34D/L30; std w/22887) | 237.65 |
| 35J/M53 | 2 speed automatic transmission | |
| | W/34A | 148.92 |
| | W/350 ci V-8; NA w/22687 | 190.00 |
| 35K/M38 | 3 speed Turbo Hydra-matic transmission | |
| | W/34A | 175.26 |
| | W/350 ci V-8 | 183.96 |
| 35L/M40 | 3 speed Turbo Hydra-matic transmission (NC w/22887) | 201.48 |
| 321/Y88 | Basic Option Group | |
| | 22387 6 cyl | 448.17 |
| | 22387 V-8 | 458.73 |
| | 22487 V-8 | 432.40 |
| | 22687 w/350 ci V-8 | 471.36 |
| | 22687 w/opt V-8s | 492.48 |
| 321/Y88 | Basic Group; AM radio only (22887) | 66.35 |
| 331/Y96 | Handling Package (22687; incl 478/P05) | 205.37 |
| 361/G80 | Safe-T-Track rear axle (std w/22887) | 46.34 |
| 368/G90-2 | Performance axle | 10.53 |
| 401/U63 | AM radio w/windshield antenna | 66.35 |
| 403/U69 | AM/FM radio & windshield antenna | 139.02 |
| 405/U58 | AM/FM stereo radio & windshield antenna (NA w/411/U80 | 239.08 |
| 411/U80 | Rear seat speaker (NA w/405/U58, 414/U55, 412/U57) | 18.96 |
| 412/U57 | 8 track stereo player (NA w/411/U80, 414/U55) | 133.76 |
| 414/U55 | Cassette tape player (NA w/411/U80, 412/U57) | 133.76 |
| 421/A90 | Remote deck lid release | 14.74 |
| 422/K45 | Dual-stage air cleaner (NA w/22887) | 9.48 |
| 424/D58 | Rear console | 26.33 |
| 431/D55 | Front console (w/floor shift only) | 58.98 |
| 432/C24 | Concealed wipers (std w/22487, 22887) | 18.96 |
| 434/D35 | Dual sport OSRV mirrors, LH remote (22387 only) | 26.33 |
| 441/D34 | RH visor vanity mirror | 3.16 |
| 451/AK1 | Custom safety belts | 15.80 |
| 461/N30 | Custom cushion steering wheel (std w/22487, 22687; NA w/22887) | 15.80 |

| 464/NK3 | Formula steering wheel | |
| | 22487, 22687 | 42.13 |
| | 22387; std w/22887 | 57.93 |
| 471/P06 | Chrome wheel trim rings (std w/22487) | 26.33 |
| 472/P02 | Custom wheel covers | |
| | 22387, 22687 | 31.60 |
| | 22487 | 5.27 |
| 474/N98 | Rally II wheels | |
| | 22387, 22687; NC w/22887 | 89.52 |
| | 22487 | 63.19 |
| 478/P05 | Honeycomb wheels | |
| | 22387, 22687 | 126.38 |
| | 22487 | 100.05 |
| | 22887 | 36.86 |
| 481/B80 | Roof drip moldings (incl w/SVT vinyl top/C08; std w/22487) | 15.80 |
| 484/B85 | Belt reveal moldings (std w/22487) | 21.06 |
| 491/B96 | Front & rear wheel opening moldings (std w/22487; NA w/22887) | 15.80 |
| 492/B93 | Door edge guards | 6.32 |
| 494/B84 | Black vinyl bodyside moldings (NA w/22887) | 31.60 |
| 501/N41 | Variable-ratio power steering (std w/22887) | 115.85 |
| 502/J50 | Power front brakes (w/22887) | 47.39 |
| 504/N33 | Tilt steering wheel (NA w/manual steering & column shift) | 45.29 |
| 521/B32 | Front floor mats only | 7.37 |
| 522/B33 | Rear floor mats only | 6.32 |
| 524/B42 | Rear compartment mat (std w/22487) | 8.43 |
| 531/A01 | Soft-Ray glass, all windows | 37.92 |
| 532/A02 | Soft-Ray glass, windshield only | 30.54 |
| 534/C49 | Electric rear window defroster (NA w/34A or 541/C50) | 63.19 |
| 541/C50 | Rear window defogger (NA w/534/C49) | 31.60 |
| 551/A31 | Power windows (required w/431/D55) | 115.85 |
| 554/AU3 | Power door locks | 45.29 |
| 572/D80 | Deck lid spoiler (std w/22887; available w/22687) | 32.65 |
| 582/C60 | Custom AC (NA w/34A) | 407.59 |
| 601/WU3 | Hood air inlet (available w/455 HO engine only on 22687) | 84.26 |
| 652/W74 | Warning & clock lamps (NA w/714/U30, 718/W63, 722/U35) | 42.13 |
| 654/TP1 | Delco X battery (w/455 ci V-8 only) | 26.33 |
| 664/Y92 | Convenience lamps | 11.59 |
| 681/U05 | Dual horns (22387 only; std w/all others) | 4.21 |
| 684/N65 | Space-Saver spare tire | 15.80 |
| 691/WU1 | Self-charging flashlight | 12.64 |
| 692/UA1 | HD battery (NA w/582/C60) | 10.53 |
| 701/V01 | HD radiator | 21.06 |

| Sales Code/UPC | Description | Retail Price |
|---|---|---|
| 704/WT5 | Mountain performance option | |
| | W/582/C60 | 10.53 |
| | Wo/582/C60 | 31.60 |
| 714/U30 | Rally gauges, clock, instrument panel tachometer (NA w/34A, 718/W63, 722/U35, 652/W74) | 94.79 |
| 718/W63 | Rally gauges & clock (NA w/34A, 652/W74; incl 722/U35) | 47.39 |
| 722/U35 | Electric clock (incl w/652/W74, 714/U30, 718/W63) | 15.80 |
| 731/W54 | Custom trim option (std w/22487; NA w/22387) | 78.99 |
| 734/V32 | Rear bumper guards | 15.80 |
| GR/PX6 | F78-14 whitewall tires (22387, 22487) | 45.29 |
| HR/PL3 | E78-14 whitewall tires (22387, 22487) | 28.44 |
| MF/PY6 | F70-14 blackwall tires (22387, 22487) | 35.81 |
| ML/PL4 | F70-14 white-letter tires | |
| | 22387, 22487 | 76.88 |
| | 22687 | 41.07 |
| NL/PM7 | F60-15 white-letter tires | |
| | W/Rally II wheels (22687; std w/22887) | 162.19 |
| | W/honeycomb wheels (22687; std w/22887) | 199.05 |
| SVT/C08 | Cordova top | |
| | 22387, 22687 | 89.52 |
| | 22487 | 73.72 |

## Facts

Changes were minimal on the 1971 Firebirds. Nonfunctional fender louvers were located behind the wheelwells, and in the interior, high-back bucket seats replaced the previous low-back design.

A new wheel, the polycast honeycomb 15x7 in., was first seen on these Firebirds. Fourteen-inch versions were made available on other Pontiac models. Looking deceptively like aluminum, the polycast wheels' centers were painted molded urethane mounted on a steel backing. The honeycomb wheel was standard on the Trans Am, with the Rally IIs a no-cost option.

The Trans Am's rear spoiler was optionally available on the Formula.

A new version of the Pontiac V-8, the 455 ci V-8, on the Firebird. Two versions were available: the regular L75 455 rated at 325 hp and the LS5 455 HO rated at 335 hp. The HO was the standard and only engine available on the Trans Am. It came with the Ram Air IV's aluminum intake manifold and a four-bolt main cylinder block. The engine dress-up kit was not part of the engine.

The base Firebird still got the 250 ci inline six, with the L30 350 ci V-8 two-barrel optional. The Esprit standard engine was upgraded to the L30, with the L65 400 ci V-8 two-barrel optional.

The Formula got the L30 350 ci V–8 standard, with the L78 400 ci V–8 four-barrel optional. Both 455s were optional on the Formula too.

The Y96 handling package, available for the Formula, included the honeycomb wheels with F60x15 raised white-letter tires and the Trans Am's front and rear sway bars and rear springs.

A new rear console that included an ashtray and seatbelt buckle receptacles was available under option D58.

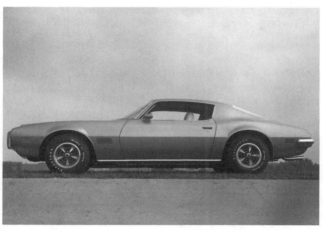

*1971 Firebird Formula 400*

# Chapter 6

# 1972 Firebird

## Production

| Model | Manual | Automatic | Total |
|---|---|---|---|
| 2 dr base 6 cyl | | | 2,975 |
| 2 dr base 8 cyl | 2,778* | 20,244* | 20,047 |
| 2 dr Esprit 8 cyl | 947 | 19,238 | 20,185 |
| 2 dr Formula 400 8 cyl | 1,860 | 5,942 | 7,802 |
| 2 dr Trans Am 8 cyl | 885 | 1,231 | 2,116 |
| Total | 6,470 | 46,655 | 53,125 |

*Includes six- and eight-cylinders.

## Serial Numbers

**Description**
2S87T2N500001
2—Pontiac
S—Firebird body series (S = base, T = Esprit, U = Formula,
V = Trans Am)
87—body style (87 = 2 dr coupe)
T—engine code
2—last digit of model year (2 = 1972)
N—assembly plant (N = Norwood)
500001—consecutive sequence number

**Location**
On plate attached to left side of dash, visible through windshield.

## Engine VIN Codes
D—250 ci
M—350 ci 2V single exhaust
N—350 ci 2V dual exhaust
R—400 ci 4V single exhaust
T—400 ci 4V dual exhaust
X—455 ci 4V dual exhaust

## Engine Identification Codes
CBA, CBG—250 ci I-6 1 bbl 110 hp manual
CBC, CBJ—250 ci I-6 1 bbl 110 hp automatic
WR—350 ci V-8 2 bbl 175 hp manual
YR—350 ci V-8 2 bbl 175 hp automatic
YX, YZ—400 ci V-8 2 bbl 200 hp automatic
ZX—400 ci V-8 2 bbl 200 hp automatic Calif

WK—400 ci V-8 4 bbl 250 hp 4 speed manual
YS, YT—400 ci V-8 4 bbl 250 hp automatic
WD, WM—455 ci V-8 4 bbl 300 hp manual
YB, YE—455 ci V-8 4 bbl 300 hp automatic

## Carburetors
350 ci 175 hp manual—WGD 488062 (6311S)
350 ci 175 hp automatic—7042062
400 ci 200 hp automatic—7042060, 7042062 (ZX)
400 ci 250 hp manual—7042263
400 ci 250 hp automatic—7042272 (YT)
455 ci 300 hp manual—7042273
455 ci 300 hp automatic—7042270

## Head Castings
350 ci 175 hp—7H1
400 ci 200 hp—7J2
400 ci 250 hp—7K3
455 ci 300 hp—7F6

## Exterior Color Codes

| Color | Code | Color | Code |
|---|---|---|---|
| Cameo White | 11 | Monarch Yellow | 56 |
| Revere Silver | 14 | Brasilia Gold | 57 |
| Adriatic Blue | 24 | Anaconda Gold | 63 |
| Lucerne Blue | 26 | Sundance Orange | 65 |
| Julep Green | 36 | Cardinal Red | 75 |
| Springfield Green | 43 | | |
| Wilderness Green | 48 | | |
| Brittany Beige | 50 | | |
| Quezal Gold | 53 | | |
| Shadow Gold | 55 | | |

## Interior Trim Codes

| Color | Std Buckets | Custom Buckets |
|---|---|---|
| Blue | — | 211 |
| Ivory | 121 | 221 |
| Saddle | 131 | 231 |
| Green | 141 | 241 |
| Beige (Covert) | — | 251/351* |
| Black | 161 | 261/361* |

*Cloth/vinyl.

## Vinyl Top Color Codes
| | |
|---|---|
| Black | 2 |
| Blue | 3 |
| Parchment | 5 |
| Fawn | 8 |
| Green | 9 |

## Options

| Sales Code/UPC | Description | Retail Price |
|---|---|---|
| | 2 dr coupe | $2,828.00 |
| | 2 dr coupe Esprit | 3,194.00 |
| | 2 dr coupe Formula | 3,221.00 |
| | 2 dr coupe Trans Am | 4,256.00 |
| 34H/L30 | 350 ci V-8 2V engine (base) | 118.00 |
| 34R/L30 | 350 ci V-8 2V engine (Calif; 35K/M38 required w/base) | 118.00 |
| 34R/L65 | 400 ci V-8 2V engine (Esprit w/35L/M40 only) | 51.00 |
| 34S/L78 | 400 ci V-8 4V engine (Formula 400) | 97.00 |
| 34X/LS5 | 455 ci HO V-8 engine (Formula 400; required w/601/WU3, 634/K65; w/35L/M40, 35G/M22) | 231.00 |
| 35B/M02 | 3 speed manual transmission w/floor shift (base 6 cyl) | 10.00 |
| 35E/M20 | 4 speed manual transmission (exc Trans Am; w/34H/L30, 34S/L78 only) | 200.00 |
| 35G/M22 | HD 4 speed manual transmission (Formula 400 w/34S/L78, 34X/LS5 only) | 231.00 |
| 35J/M35 | 2 speed automatic transmission (NA Calif) | |
| | Base w/34D | 174.00 |
| | Base, Esprit wo/34D | 185.00 |
| 35K/M38 | Turbo Hydra-matic transmission | |
| | Base, Esprit, Formula 400 wo/34D | 215.00 |
| | Base w/34D | 205.00 |
| 35L/M40 | Turbo Hydra-matic transmission (Esprit, Formula 400 wo/34D, 34H/L30 | 236.00 |
| 361/G80 | Safe-T-Track differential (exc Trans Am) | 45.00 |
| 368/G92 | Performance axle | 10.00 |
| 401/U63 | AM radio | 65.00 |
| 403/U69 | AM/FM radio | 135.00 |
| 405/U58 | AM/FM stereo (incl 411/U80) | 233.00 |
| 411/U80 | Rear seat speaker | 18.00 |
| 412/U57 | Tape player (required w/401/U63, 403/U69, 405/U58) | 130.00 |
| 414/U55 | Cassette player (NA w/431/D55, 424/D58, 411/U80, 412/U57) | 130.00 |
| 423/K45 | HD air cleaner (exc Trans Am) | 9.00 |
| 424/D58 | Rear console (NA w/414/U55 w/431/D55) | 26.00 |
| 431/D55 | Front console (NA w/35A) | 57.00 |
| 432/C24 | Concealed wipers (base & Formula 400) | 18.00 |
| 434/D35 | Body-color OSRV mirror, LH remote (NA w/444/D33) | 26.00 |
| 441/D34 | RH visor vanity mirror | 3.00 |
| 442/D31 | Nonglare rearview mirror (incl w/734) | 6.00 |

| | | |
|---|---|---|
| 444/D33 | LH remote control OSRV mirror | |
| | (NA w/434/D35) | 12.00 |
| 451/AK1 | Custom front & rear shoulder belts | 15.00 |
| 461/N30 | Custom cushion steering wheel (base) | 15.00 |
| 462/N31 | Custom sport steering wheel | |
| | (incl w/332) | 56.00 |
| 464/NK3 | Formula steering wheel | |
| | Base w/501/N41 only | 56.00 |
| | Esprit, Formula 400 | 41.00 |
| 471/P06 | Custom wheel trim rings | |
| | (incl w/474/N98, 332) | 26.00 |
| 472/P02 | Custom finned wheel covers | |
| | Base, Formula 400 wo/332, 474/N98, | |
| | 478/P05 | 50.00 |
| | Esprit | 24.00 |
| 474/N98 | Rally II wheels | 87.00 |
| 476/P01 | Deluxe wheel covers | |
| | Base, Formula 400, NA w/332 | 31.00 |
| | Esprit | 5.00 |
| 478/P05 | Honeycomb wheels | |
| | Base, Formula 400 | 123.00 |
| | Esprit | 97.00 |
| 481/B80 | Roof drip moldings (exc Esprit) | 15.00 |
| 484/B85 | Belt reveal moldings (exc Trans Am, | |
| | required w/582/C60 w/534/C49 | 15.00 |
| 491/B96 | Front & rear wheel opening moldings | |
| | (base & Formula 400 only) | 21.00 |
| 492/B93 | Door edge guards | 6.00 |
| 494/B84 | Vinyl bodyside moldings (exc Trans Am) | 31.00 |
| 501/N41 | Variable-ratio power steering | |
| | (exc Trans Am; required | |
| | w/582/C60 w/534/C49) | 113.00 |
| 502/JL2 | Power front disc brakes | |
| | (std in Trans Am) | 46.00 |
| 504/N33 | Tilt steering (required w/501/N41; | |
| | NA w/35J/M35, 35K/M38, 35L/M40 | |
| | or wo/431/D55) | 44.00 |
| 521/B32 | Front throw mats | 7.00 |
| 522/B33 | Rear throw mats | 6.00 |
| 524/B42 | Trunk mat (incl in 724/Y90) | 8.00 |
| 531/A01 | Tinted glass, all windows | 37.00 |
| 532/A02 | Tinted glass, windshield | 30.00 |
| 534/C49 | Electric rear window defogger | |
| | (NA w/34D, 541/C50) | 62.00 |
| 541/C50 | Rear window defogger (NA w/534/C49) | 31.00 |
| 551/A31 | Power windows (required w/431/D55) | 113.00 |
| 554/AU3 | Power door locks | 44.00 |
| 582/C60 | Manual AC | 397.00 |
| 591/VJ9 | Calif test (required on Calif cars) | 15.00 |
| 601/WU3 | Hood inlet (Formula 400 | |
| | requires 34X/L55) | 56.00 |
| 611/D80 | Rear air spoiler (Formula 400 only) | 32.00 |

| Sales Code/UPC | Description | Retail Price |
|---|---|---|
| 614/D98 | Vinyl stripes (NA w/494/B84, Trans Am) | 41.00 |
| 634/K65 | Unitized ignition (required w/34X/L55 on Formula 400) | 77.00 |
| 681/U05 | Dual horns (base) | 4.00 |
| 684/N65 | Space-Saver spare tire (wo/474/N98, 478/P05) | 13.00 |
| 692/UA1 | HD battery (NA w/582/C60) | 10.00 |
| 701/V01 | HD radiator | 21.00 |
| 714/U30 | Rally gauge w/tachometer & clock (NA w/34D, 722/U35, 718/W63) | 92.00 |
| 718/W63 | Rally gauge cluster w/clock (NA w/34D, 722/U35) | 46.00 |
| 722/U35 | Electric clock | 15.00 |
| 724/Y90 | Custom Trim Group (Formula 400, Trans Am) | 77.00 |
| 731/V30 | Front & rear bumper guards | 25.00 |
| SPS/W51 | Solid special paint (exc Trans Am) | |
| | W/vinyl top | 97.00 |
| | Wo/vinyl top | 113.00 |
| SVT/C08 | Cordova vinyl top | |
| | Esprit | 72.00 |
| | Base, Formula 400 | 87.00 |
| TGR/PX6 | F78-14 whitewall fiberglass tires (base, Esprit) | 44.00 |
| THR/PL | E78-14 whitewall fiberglass tires (base, Esprit) | 28.00 |
| TMF/PY6 | F70-14 black fiberglass tires (base, Esprit) | 35.00 |
| TML/PL4 | F70-14 white-letter fiberglass tires | |
| | Base, Esprit | 75.00 |
| | Formula 400 | 40.00 |
| TNL/Y99 | Formula Handling Package | 87.00 |
| —/Y92 | Convenience Lamp Group | 11.00 |

## Facts

The 1972 Firebirds were similar in appearance to the 1971 models. One difference was the hex mesh on the grille, replacing the square mesh of 1970-71. The nonfunctional fender extractors used on all 1971 Firebirds—except the Trans Am—were deleted.

Engine availability was unchanged from that in 1971, though horsepower ratings were altered.

The honeycomb wheels were now available in 14 in. sizes. The 15 in. honeycombs became optional on the Trans Am. Standard were the Rally II wheels.

The Y99 handling package that was optional on the Formula did not include the honeycomb wheels. Mandatory with the optional 455 HO engine on the Formula were electronic ignition and the functional Ram Air hood. The 455 HO was the only engine available on the Trans Am.

The two-speed Powerglide automatic was phased out during the year.

The Formula steering wheel became optional on all base and Esprit Firebirds.

Firebirds were built in only one location, the Norwood facility. This would continue until 1978, when the Van Nuys plant again assembled them.

*1972 Firebird Esprit*

# 1973 Firebird

## Production

| Model | Manual | Automatic | Total |
|---|---|---|---|
| 2 dr base 6 & 8 cyl | | | 14,096 |
| 2 dr Esprit 8 cyl | | | 17,249 |
| 2 dr Formula 8 cyl | | | 10,123 |
| 2 dr Formula SD 455 8 cyl | | | 43 |
| 2 dr Trans Am 8 cyl | 1,420 | 3,130 | 4,550 |
| 2 dr Trans Am SD 455 8 cyl | 72 | 180 | 252 |
| Total | | | 46,313 |

## Serial Numbers

**Description**
2S87T3N100001
2—Pontiac
S—Firebird body series (S = base, T = Esprit, U = Formula,
  V = Trans Am)
87—body style (87 = 2 dr coupe)
T—engine code
3—last digit of model year (3 = 1973)
N—assembly plant (N = Norwood)
100001—consecutive sequence number

**Location**
On plate attached to left side of dash, visible through windshield.

## Engine VIN Codes
D—250 ci
M—350 ci 2V single exhaust
N—350 ci 2V dual exhaust
P—400 ci 2V dual exhaust
R—400 ci 2V single exhaust
S—400 ci 4V single exhaust
T—400 ci 4V dual exhaust
X—455 ci 4V dual exhaust
Y—455 ci 4V dual exhaust

## Engine Identification Codes
CCC, CCD—250 ci I-6 1 bbl 100 hp manual
CCA, CCB—250 ci I-6 1 bbl 100 hp automatic
YL, YR, ZR, ZT—350 ci V-8 2 bbl 150 hp automatic
XR—350 ci V-8 2 bbl 175 hp manual
YZ, ZK, ZX—400 ci V-8 2 bbl 170 hp automatic

YX—400 ci V-8 2 bbl 185 hp automatic
Y6, WP, WS, YG—400 ci V-8 4 bbl 230 hp manual
Y3, XN, YS—400 ci V-8 4 bbl 230 hp automatic
WT, WW—455 ci V-8 4 bbl 250 hp manual
X7, XM, YD, YK—455 ci V-8 4 bbl 250 hp automatic
XE, XL, YA, YC—455 ci V-8 4 bbl 250 hp automatic
ZJ—455 ci V-8 4 bbl 290 hp manual SD 455
XD—455 ci V-8 4 bbl 290 hp automatic SD 455

## Carburetors
350 ci 150 hp automatic—7043062, 7043063, 7043072
350 ci 175 hp manual—7043071
400 ci 170 hp automatic—7043061 AIR, 7043070
400 ci 185 hp automatic—7043060, 7043061
400 ci 230 hp manual—7043263, 7043264
455 ci 250 hp manual—7043265
455 ci 250 hp automatic—7043262, 7043272
455 ci 290 hp manual—7043273
455 ci 290 hp automatic—7043270

## Head Castings
350 ci 150/175 hp—46
400 ci 170 hp—4C, 4X
400 ci 185/230 hp—4X
455 ci 250 hp—4X
455 ci 290 hp—16/485216

## Exterior Color Codes

| | | | |
|---|---|---|---|
| Cameo White | 11 | Sunlight Yellow | 51 |
| Porcelain Blue | 24 | Desert Sand | 56 |
| Regatta Blue | 26 | Valencia Gold | 60 |
| Admiralty Blue | 29 | Ascot Silver | 64 |
| Verdant Green | 42 | Burma Brown | 68 |
| Slate Green | 44 | Florentine Red | 74 |
| Golden Olive | 46 | Buccaneer Red | 75 |
| Brewster Green | 48 | Navajo Orange | 97 |

## Interior Trim Codes

| Color | Std Buckets | Opt Custom Buckets |
|---|---|---|
| White | 321 | 421 |
| Saddle | 331 | 431 |
| Black | 361 | 461 |
| Burgundy | — | 471 |
| Beige | — | 551 |

## Vinyl Top Color Codes

| | | | |
|---|---|---|---|
| White | 1 | Green | 5 |
| Black | 2 | Dark Burgundy | 6 |
| Beige | 3 | Blue | 7 |
| Chamois | 4 | | |

# Options

| UPC | Description | Retail Price |
|-----|-------------|--------------|
| | 2 dr coupe | $2,895.00 |
| | 2 dr coupe Esprit | 3,245.00 |
| | 2 dr coupe Formula | 3,276.00 |
| | 2 dr coupe Trans Am | 4,204.00 |
| AK1 | Custom seatbelts | 15.00 |
| AU3 | Electric door locks | 44.00 |
| AV6 | Electric door locks | 44.00 |
| A01 | Tinted glass, all windows | 37.00 |
| A02 | Tinted glass, windshield | 30.00 |
| A31 | Power windows | 75.00 |
| B32 | Front floor mats | 7.00 |
| B33 | Rear floor mats | 6.00 |
| B42 | Trunk mat | 8.00 |
| B80 | Roof drip moldings | 15.00 |
| B84 | Bodyside moldings | 31.00 |
| B85 | Window & rear hood moldings | 21.00 |
| B93 | Door edge guards | 6.00 |
| B96 | Front & rear wheelhouse moldings | 15.00 |
| C08 | Cordova top | 72.00-87.00 |
| C24 | Concealed windshield wipers | 18.00 |
| C49 | Electric rear defogger | 62.00 |
| C50 | Rear defogger | 31.00 |
| C60 | Custom AC | 397.00 |
| D34 | RH visor vanity mirror | 3.00 |
| D35 | Dual body-color OSRV mirror | 26.00 |
| D55 | Front console | 57.00 |
| D58 | Rear console | 26.00 |
| D80 | Rear deck lid spoiler | 32.00 |
| D98 | Accent stripes | 41.00 |
| G80 | Safe-T-Track rear axle | 45.00 |
| G92 | Performance axle | 10.00 |
| JL2 | Power disc brakes | 46.00 |
| K05 | Engine block heater | 10.00 |
| K45 | HD air cleaner | 9.00 |
| K65 | Unitized ignition | 77.00 |
| LS2 | SD 455 V-8 4 bbl engine | 521.00-675.00 |
| L30 | 350 ci V-8 2 bbl engine | 118.00 |
| L65 | 400 ci V-8 2 bbl engine | 51.00 |
| L75 | 455 ci V-8 4 bbl engine | 154.00 |
| L78 | 400 ci V-8 4 bbl engine | 97.00 |
| M12 | 3 speed manual transmission w/floor shift | NC |
| M21 | Close-ratio 4 speed manual transmission | 200.00 |
| M20 | 4 speed manual transmission | 200.00 |
| M38 | Turbo Hydra-matic transmission | 205.00-215.00 |
| NK3 | Formula steering wheel | 41.00-56.00 |
| N30 | Custom cushion steering wheel | 15.00 |
| N33 | Tilt steering wheel | 44.00 |
| N41 | Variable-ratio power steering | 113.00 |
| N65 | Space-Saver spare tire | 15.00 |

| | | |
|---|---|---|
| N98 | Rally II wheels | 61.00–87.00 |
| PL3 | E78-14 whitewall fiberglass tires | 22.40–28.00 |
| PL4 | F70-14 white-letter fiberglass tires | 32.00–75.00 |
| PX5 | F78-14 blackwall fiberglass tires | 11.20–14.00 |
| PX6 | F78-14 whitewall fiberglass tires | 24.00–44.00 |
| PY6 | F70-14 blackwall fiberglass tires | 16.80–35.00 |
| P01 | Deluxe wheel covers | 26.00 |
| P02 | Custom finned wheel covers (Esprit) | 24.00–50.00 |
| P05 | Honeycomb wheels | 97.00–123.00 |
| P06 | Wheel trim rings | 26.00 |
| P85 | GR70-14 whitewall steel-belted radial tires | 56.00–70.00 |
| TP1 | Maintenance-free battery | 26.00 |
| UA1 | HD battery | 10.00 |
| U01 | HD radiator | 21.00 |
| U05 | Dual horns | 4.00 |
| U35 | Electric clock | 15.00 |
| U57 | Stereo tape player | 130.00 |
| U58 | AM/FM stereo | 233.00 |
| U63 | AM radio | 65.00 |
| U69 | AM/FM radio | 135.00 |
| U80 | Rear speaker | 18.00 |
| WU3 | Ram Air hood | 56.00 |
| WW7 | Trans Am hood decal | 55.00 |
| WW8 | Rally gauges w/tachometer | 92.00 |
| W63 | Rally gauges w/clock | 46.00 |
| Y88 | Basic Option Group | 65.00–480.00 |
| Y90 | Custom Trim Group | 77.00 |
| Y92 | Lamp Group | 10.00 |
| Y95 | Body Protection Group | 52.00 |
| Y99 | Formula Handling Package (Formula only) | 72.60–157.00 |
| 24F | Bright Blue carpet | NC |
| 75F | Red carpet | NC |
| 97F | Orange carpet | NC |
| Std | 6 cyl engine | NC |

## Facts

Differences again were slight on the 1973 Firebird. Looking outwardly the same, its Endura bumper was strengthened to withstand the new 5 mph standards. At the same time, the grille was recessed less deeply and the valance panel incorporated a small spoiler. The grille had an open square mesh. In the rear, the bumper was repositioned outward 2.5 in. and strengthened to withstand the 2.5 mph rear standard.

In the interior, the simulated wood on the dash panel was changed to resemble an African crossfire mahogany, and the lower door panels were no longer carpeted.

Color selection expanded on the Trans Am. In addition to the Cameo White, Brewster Green and Buccaneer Red were available;

however, Lucerne Blue was deleted. The new, large WW7 Trans Am hood decal became an option on the Trans Am. The bird decal was black, but its background color varied depending on the Trans Am's exterior color. It was orange on Buccaneer Red, blue with Cameo White and light green on Brewster Green cars. The Trans Am fender decals were larger, and engine size decals, either 455 or SD 455, were located on the shaker scoop, which was nonfunctional. The Formula's Ram Air hood was also nonfunctional.

The big deal for 1973 was the Super Duty (SD) 455 ci V-8 that was optional on the Formula and Trans Am. It came with a reinforced four-bolt main block that had provision for dry-sump oiling and with forged steel connecting rods—as opposed to the cast rods on regular Pontiac engines. The cylinder heads featured round exhaust ports and complementary exhaust manifolds. Early engines were rated at 310 hp, whereas later versions were rated at 290 hp owing to internal changes, mainly in the camshaft specs, to meet emissions standards.

The Trans Am's steering box got a new ratio that resulted in 2.41 wheel turns lock to lock. Previously it gave 2.5 turns. The rear sway bar size was reduced to 0.812 in. In addition to the standard F60x15 raised white-letter tires on Rally II rims, GR70x15 radials were optionally available.

A new optional side tape stripe was available on the base, Esprit and Formula models.

The 1973 manual-equipped Firebirds had a smaller clutch pedal and pad for additional left-foot room.

*1973 Firebird*

# Chapter 8

# 1974 Firebird

## Production

| Model | Manual | Automatic | Total |
|---|---|---|---|
| 2 dr base 6 cyl | | | 7,603 |
| 2 dr base 8 cyl | | | 18,769 |
| 2 dr Esprit 8 cyl | | | 22,583 |
| 2 dr Formula 8 cyl | | | 14,461 |
| 2 dr Formula SD 455 8 cyl | | | 58 |
| 2 dr Trans Am w/400 ci 8 cyl | 1,750 | 2,914 | 4,664 |
| 2 dr Trans Am w/455 ci 8 cyl | — | 4,648 | 4,648 |
| 2 dr Trans Am SD 455 8 cyl | 212 | 731 | 943 |
| Total | | | 73,729 |

## Serial Numbers

**Description**
2S87T4N100001
2—Pontiac
S—Firebird body series (S = base, T = Esprit, U = Formula,
V = Trans Am)
87—body style (87 = 2 dr coupe)
T—engine code
4—last digit of model year (4 = 1974)
N—assembly plant (N = Norwood)
100001—consecutive sequence number

**Location**
   On plate attached to left side of dash, visible through windshield.

## Engine VIN Codes
D—250 ci
M—350 ci 2V single exhaust          S—400 ci 4V single exhaust
N—350 ci 2V dual exhaust            T—400 ci 4V dual exhaust
P—400 ci 2V dual exhaust            X—455 ci 4V dual exhaust
R—400 ci 2V single exhaust          Y—455 ci 4V dual exhaust

## Engine Identification Codes
CJA, CJB, CJC—250 ci I-6 1 bbl 100 hp manual or automatic
WA—350 ci V-8 2 bbl 155 hp manual
YA—350 ci V-8 2 bbl 155 hp automatic
ZA—350 ci V-8 2 bbl 155 hp automatic
AA—350 ci V-8 2 bbl 155 hp automatic
ZA—350 ci V-8 2 bbl 170 hp automatic
AD, AH, YF, YH—400 ci V-8 2 bbl 190 hp automatic

ZJ, ZK—400 ci V-8 2 bbl 190 hp automatic
Y3, WR, WT—400 ci V-8 4 bbl 200 hp manual
A3, YL, YM, YT—400 ci V-8 4 bbl 200 hp automatic
AT, YZ, ZS, ZT—400 ci V-8 4 bbl 200 hp automatic
A4, Y9, Z4, YY—455 ci V-8 4 bbl 250 hp automatic
AU, YW, ZU, ZW—455 ci V-8 4 bbl 250 hp automatic
W8—455 ci V-8 4 bbl 290 hp manual SD 455
Y8—455 ci V-8 4 bbl 290 hp automatic SD 455

## Carburetors
350 ci 155 hp manual—7044071
350 ci 155 hp automatic (YA)—7043062
350 ci 155 hp automatic (AA)—7043072
350 ci 155/170 hp automatic—7044063 AIR
400 ci 190 hp automatic (YF, YH)—7044066
400 ci 190 hp automatic (AD, AH)—7043070
400 ci 190 hp automatic (ZJ, ZK)—7044067
400 ci 200 hp automatic (YL, YM, YT, ZS, ZT)—7044266
400 ci 200 hp automatic (A3, AT)—7044274
400 ci 225 hp manual—7043263
455 ci 250 hp automatic—7044262, 7044272 (AU)
455 ci 290 hp manual—7044273
455 ci 290 hp automatic—7044270

## Head Castings
350 ci 155/170 hp (WA, ZA)—4C
350 ci 155 hp (AA, YA)—46
400 ci 190 hp (ZJ)—4C
400 ci all others—4X
455 ci 250 hp—4X
455 ci 290 hp—16 (6H)

## Exterior Color Codes

| Cameo White | 11 |
| Regatta Blue | 26 |
| Admiralty Blue | 29 |
| Gulfmist Aqua | 36 |
| Fernmist Green | 40 |
| Limefire Green | 46 |
| Pinemist Green | 49 |
| Carmel Beige | 50 |
| Sunstorm Yellow | 51 |
| Denver Gold | 53 |
| Colonial Gold | 55 |
| Crestwood Brown | 59 |
| Ascot Silver | 64 |
| Fire Coral Bronze | 66 |
| Honduras Maroon | 74 |
| Buccaneer Red | 75 |

## Interior Trim Codes

**Standard**

| Color | Vinyl Buckets |
| --- | --- |
| White | 721 |
| Saddle | 731 |
| Black | 761 |
| White/Blue seats | 721/335 |
| White/Green seats | 721/336 |
| White/Red seats | 721/338 |
| Black/White seats | 761/331 |
| Black/Red seats | 761/338 |

#### Optional

| Color | Vinyl Buckets | | |
|---|---|---|---|
| Blue | 811 | Green/White seats | 941/331 |
| Red | 901 | Black/White seats | 961/331 |
| White | 921 | Black/Red seats | 961/333 |
| Green | 941 | Black/Red trim | 861/338 |
| Saddle | 931/831* | White/Blue trim | 921/335 |
| Black | 961/861* | White/Green trim | 921/336 |
| Blue/White seats | 811/331 | White/Red trim | 921/338 |
| Red/White seats | 901/331 | Black/Red trim | 961/338 |
| Red/Black seats | 901/332 | *Cloth/vinyl. | |

## Vinyl Top Color Codes

| | |
|---|---|
| White | 1 |
| Black | 2 |
| Beige | 3 |
| Chamois | 4 |
| Green | 5 |
| Blue | 7 |

## Options

| Sales Code | Description | Retail Price |
|---|---|---|
| | 2 dr coupe | $3,335.00 |
| | 2 dr coupe Esprit | 3,687.00 |
| | 2 dr coupe Formula | 3,659.00 |
| | 2 dr coupe Trans Am | 4,446.00 |
| 35D | 250 ci 6 cyl engine (S87) | Std |
| 35M | 350 ci 2V engine (std w/T87, U87; NA w/V87) | 118.00 |
| 35R | 400 ci 2V engine (NA w/S87, V87; w/36L only) | 51.00 |
| 35S | 400 ci 4V engine (w/36L, 36E only; NA w/S87, T87) | 97.00 |
| 35W | 455 ci 4V engine | |
| | V87 price only | 57.00 |
| | U87 price only; 36L required | 154.00 |
| 35X | SD 455 engine (required w/36E, 36L) | |
| | V87 price only | 578.00 |
| | U87 price only | 675.00 |
| 36B | 3 speed manual transmission w/floor shift (w/35D, 35M only) | NC |
| 36E | 4 speed manual transmission (NA w/35D, 35R, 35W) | 207.00 |
| 36K | M38 Turbo Hydra-matic transmission | |
| | W/S87 6 cyl | 221.00 |
| | W/T87, U87 | 211.00 |
| 36L | M40 Turbo Hydra-matic transmission (NA w/587; std w/V87) | 242.00 |
| 308 | Custom Trim Package | 77.00 |

| Sales Code | Description | Retail Price |
|---|---|---|
| 371 | Safe-T-Track axle (std w/V87) | 45.00 |
| 378 | Performance axle (required w/682 w/manual transmission | 10.00 |
| 411 | Push-button AM radio | 65.00 |
| 413 | AM/FM radio | 135.00 |
| 415 | AM/FM stereo | 233.00 |
| 421 | Rear speaker (NA w/415, 422; 411 or 413 required) | 21.00 |
| 422 | 8 track stereo player (431 w/411, 413 or 415 required) | 130.00 |
| 424 | Rear console | 26.00 |
| 431 | Front console (NA w/36A) | 58.00 |
| 432 | Concealed wipers (std w/T87, V87) | 18.00 |
| 434 | Dual sport mirrors (std w/T87, U87, V87) | 26.00 |
| 441 | RH vanity mirror | 3.00 |
| 461 | Custom cushion steering wheel (std w/T87 U87; NA w/V87) | 15.00 |
| 464 | Formula steering wheel (501 required) | |
| | Std w/V87 | 41.00 |
| | S87 | 56.00 |
| 471 | Wheel trim rings (std w/V87; NA w/T87) | 26.00 |
| 472 | Custom finned wheel cover | |
| | T87 | 24.00 |
| | NA w/V87 | 50.00 |
| 474 | Rally II wheel rims | |
| | S87 & U87 wo/684 | 87.00 |
| | U87 w/684 | 74.80 |
| | T87 | 61.00 |
| 476 | Deluxe wheel covers (std w/T87; NA w/V87) | 26.00 |
| 478 | Honeycomb wheel rims | |
| | S87 & U87 wo/684 | 123.00 |
| | U87 w/684 | 103.00 |
| | T87 | 97.00 |
| 481 | Roof drip moldings (std w/T87) | 15.00 |
| 484 | Window sill & roof hood edge moldings (std w/T87) | 21.00 |
| 491 | Wheel opening moldings (std w/T87; NA w/V87) | 15.00 |
| 492 | Door edge guards | 6.00 |
| 494 | Black vinyl bodyside moldings (NA w/V87) | 31.00 |
| 502 | Power front disc brakes (required w/35X) | 46.00 |
| 504 | Tilt steering wheel (NA w/column shift Hydra-matic) | 45.00 |
| 511 | Custom pedal trim plates (std w/T87) | 5.00 |
| 512 | V87 hood decal (V87 only) | 55.00 |
| 514 | Ram Air hood (U87 w/35S only; incl w/35X; std w/V87) | 56.00 |
| 541 | Calif emissions test (required w/Calif cars) | 20.00 |
| 551 | Power windows (w/431 only) | 78.00 |
| 554 | Electric door locks | 46.00 |

| | | |
|---|---|---|
| 571 | Soft-Ray glass, all windows | 38.00 |
| 572 | Soft-Ray glass, windshield only | 31.00 |
| 574 | Maintenance-free battery (NA w/591) | 26.00 |
| 582 | Custom AC (NA w/35D) | 446.00 |
| 591 | HD battery (NA w/574) | 10.00 |
| 592 | Electric rear window defroster (NA w/35D, 594) | 64.00 |
| 594 | Rear window defogger (NA w/592) | 33.00 |
| 601 | Engine block heater (NA w/35D) | 10.00 |
| 602 | Unitized ignition (w/35S, 35W only; NA w/S87, T87) | 77.00 |
| 604 | HD dual-stage air cleaner (NA w/V87, 35X) | 9.00 |
| 614 | Trunk mat (std w/custom buckets & T87) | 8.00 |
| 622 | Front floot mats | 7.00 |
| 624 | Rear floor mats | 6.00 |
| 638 | Vinyl tape stripes (NA w/V87) | 41.00 |
| 654 | Lamp Package (luggage, glovebox, instrument panel courtesy) | 10.00 |
| 681 | Rear air spoiler (std w/V87; NA w/T87) | NA |
| 682 | Dual exhaust (NA w/35D; std w/U87, V87) | 45.00 |
| 684 | Space-Saver spare tire | NA |
| 691 | Custom front & rear seatbelts & shoulder straps | 15.00 |
| 694 | Dual horns (S87 only; std w/other Firebirds) | 4.00 |
| 711 | Electric clock (incl w/V87, 712, 714) | 15.00 |
| 712 | Rally gauges & clock (NA w/711, V87) | 46.00 |
| 714 | Rally gauges w/clock & tachometer (NA w/711, 712; std w/V87) | 92.00 |
| 722 | HD radiator (NA w/582) | 21.00 |
| 734 | Impact protection bumper | 5.00 |
| 804 | Kmph speedometer | Std |
| SVT | Vinyl top | |
| | T87 | 72.00 |
| | S87, U87, V87 | 87.00 |
| TGF | F78–14 blackwall fiberglass tires (base, Esprit; wo/582) | |
| | Wo/684 | 14.00 |
| | W/684 | 11.20 |
| TGJ | Radial tuned suspension | |
| | T87 wo/582, 684 | 145.00 |
| | T87 w/582, 684 | 119.00 |
| | T87 w/582, wo/684 | 131.00 |
| | T87 w/582, w/684 | 107.80 |
| | U87 wo/684 | 30.00 |
| | U87 w/684 | 24.00 |
| TGK | Radial tuned suspension (S87 or T87) | |
| | Wo/582, 684 | 155.00 |
| | W/582, 684 | 127.00 |
| | W/582, wo/684 | 141.00 |
| | W/582, w/684 | 115.80 |
| TGR | F78–14 whitewall tires (base, Esprit) | |
| | Wo/582, 684 | 44.00 |

| Sales Code | Description | Retail Price |
| --- | --- | --- |
| | W/582, 684 | 35.20 |
| | W/582, wo/684 | 30.00 |
| | W/582, 684 | 24.00 |
| THB | E78-14 tires w/white lettering (base, Esprit) | |
| | Wo/582, 684 | 28.00 |
| | W/684 | 22.40 |
| TML | F70-14 blackwall tires w/white lettering (base, Esprit) | |
| | Wo/582, 684 | 75.00 |
| | W/582, wo/684 | 61.00 |
| | Wo/582, w/684 | 60.00 |
| | W/684, 582 | 48.80 |
| TVH | GR-70x15 steel radial tires (Formula) | |
| | W/684 | 40.00 |
| | Wo/684 | 50.00 |
| TVK | GR70-15 steel radial tires w/white lettering | |
| | Base, Esprit wo/684 | 92.00 |
| | Base, Esprit w/684 | 73.60 |
| | Trans Am wo/684 | 42.00 |
| | Trans Am w/684 | 33.60 |

## Facts

The 1974 Firebird got a new front end treatment with a slanted grille known as the soft nose. In the rear, wider, larger taillights were used, and a soft, wraparound bumper.

Variable-ratio power steering became standard equipment on all Firebirds.

The Trans Am's rear spoiler also became available on the base and Esprit models.

Color choices on the Trans Am remained three: Cameo White, Buccaneer Red and Admiralty Blue, which replaced Brewster Green.

Engine availability was unchanged on the base Firebird and Esprit. The standard engine on the Formula was a 350 ci V-8 two-barrel rated at 170 hp. Optional were the two 400 ci V-8s, rated at 190 and 225 hp, and the two 455s. The regular version, L75, was rated at 250 hp, and the LS2 SD 455 was rated at 290 hp.

Standard on the Trans Am was the 400 ci V-8 225 hp, with the regular 455 and SD 455 optional. The L75 455 was available only with the Turbo Hydra-matic automatic. The new radial tuned suspension (RTS) system, standard on the Trans Am and all Firebirds, necessitated the use of GR70x15 steel-belted radials. Rally II wheels were standard.

The 400 ci and 455 ci V-8s got GM's new HEI electronic ignition.

This was the last year for dual exhausts on the second-generation Firebirds.

The 455 and SD 455 were dropped after the 1974 model year.

*1974 Firebird Formula 400*

# Chapter 9

# 1975 Firebird

## Production

| Model | Manual | Automatic | Total |
|---|---|---|---|
| 2 dr base 6 & 8 cyl | | | 22,293 |
| 2 dr Esprit 6 & 8 cyl | | | 20,826 |
| 2 dr Formula 8 cyl | | | 13,670 |
| 2 dr Trans Am w/400 ci 8 cyl | 6,140 | 20,277 | 26,417 |
| 2 dr Trans Am w/455 ci 8 cyl | 857 | — | 857 |
| Total | | | 84,063 |

## Serial Numbers

**Description**
2S87W5N100001
2—Pontiac
S—Firebird body series (S = base, T = Esprit, U = Formula,
  V = Trans Am)
87—body style (87 = 2 dr coupe)
W—engine code
5—last digit of model year (5 = 1975)
N—assembly plant (N = Norwood)
100001—consecutive sequence number

**Location**
On plate attached to left side of dash, visible through windshield.

## Engine VIN Codes

D—250 ci
H—350 ci 4V
M—350 ci 2V
R—400 ci 4V
S—400 ci 4V
W—455 ci 4V

## Engine Identification Codes

JL, JT, JU—250 ci I-6 1 bbl 100 hp manual or automatic
YB—350 ci V-8 2 bbl 155 hp automatic
YN, YO—350 ci V-8 4 bbl 175 hp manual
ZP—350 ci V-8 4 bbl 175 hp automatic
WT—400 ci V-8 4 bbl 185 hp manual
YS—400 ci V-8 4 bbl 185 hp automatic
WX—455 ci V-8 4 bbl 200 hp manual

## Carburetors

350 ci 155 hp—7045171
350 ci 175 hp manual—7045269
350 ci 175 hp automatic—7045268, 7045568 AIR

400 ci 185 hp manual—7045263
400 ci 185 hp automatic—7045274
455 ci 200 hp manual—7045263

## Head Casting
350, 400, 455 ci—5C

## Exterior Color Codes

| | | | |
|---|---|---|---|
| Cameo White | 11 | Carmel Beige | 50 |
| Sterling Silver | 13 | Sunstorm Yellow | 51 |
| Graystone | 15 | Sandstone | 55 |
| Arctic Blue | 24 | Ginger Brown | 58 |
| Bimini Blue | 26 | Copper Mist | 63 |
| Stellar Blue | 29 | Persimmon | 64 |
| Lakemist Green | 44 | Honduras Maroon | 74 |
| Alpine Green | 49 | Buccaneer Red | 75 |

## Standard Interior Trim Codes

| Color | Vinyl Buckets | Custom Buckets |
|---|---|---|
| White | 11V1 | 11W1 |
| Saddle | 63V1 | 63W1 |
| Black | 19V1 | 19W1 |
| Blue | — | 26W1 |
| Burgundy | — | 73W1 |
| Black/White seats | 91V1 | 91W1 |
| Saddle/ White seats | 96V1 | 96W1 |
| Blue/White seats | — | 92W1 |
| Burgundy/ White seats | — | 97W1 |
| White/Blue trim | 11V1/346 | 11W1/346 |
| White/ Burgundy trim | 11V1/347 | 11W1/347 |
| Black/ Burgundy trim | 19V1/347 | 19W1/347 |
| White/ Saddle trim | 11V1/343 | 11W1/343 |
| Burgundy/ Black trim | — | 19W1/347 |

## Vinyl Top Color

| | |
|---|---|
| White | Green |
| Black | Blue |
| Sandstone | Red |
| Cordovan | Silver |
| Burgundy | |

## Options

| Sales Code/UPC | Description | Retail Price |
|---|---|---|
| | 2 dr coupe | $3,713.00 |
| | 2 dr coupe Esprit | 3,958.00 |
| | 2 dr coupe Formula | 4,349.00 |
| | 2 dr coupe Trans Am | 4,740.00 |
| 32W/Y90 | Custom Trim Group | 81.00 |
| 36D/L22 | 250 ci 6 cyl engine (S87, T87) | NC |

| Sales Code/UPC | Description | Retail Price |
|---|---|---|
| 36E/L76 | 350 ci V–8 4V engine | |
| | S87, T87 | 180.00 |
| | U87 | NC |
| 36M/L30 | 350 ci V–8 2V engine (S87, T87) | 130.00 |
| 36S/L78 | 400 ci V–8 4V engine | |
| | U87 | 56.00 |
| | V87 | NC |
| 37B/M38 | 3 speed manual transmission w/floor shift | |
| | (S87, T87) | NC |
| 37E/M20 | 4 speed manual transmission | |
| | S87, T87 | 219.00 |
| | U87, V87 | NC |
| 37F/M21 | Close-ratio 4 speed manual transmission | |
| | (U87, V87) | NC |
| 37L/M38 | Turbo Hydra-matic transmission | |
| | S87, T87 | 237.00 |
| | U87, V87 | NC |
| 39A/QBU | FR78x15 blackwall steel-belted radial tires | |
| | (base, Esprit, Formula) | NC |
| 39B/QBX | GR70x15 blackwall steel-belted radial tires | |
| | Formula wo/Space-Saver spare | 40.00 |
| | Formula w/Space-Saver spare | 32.00 |
| | Trans Am | NC |
| 39L/QBP | FR78x15 white-letter steel-belted radial | |
| | tires (base, Esprit, Formula) | |
| | Wo/Space-Saver spare | 43.00 |
| | W/Space-Saver spare | 34.40 |
| 39M/QCY | GR70x15 white-letter steel-belted radial tires | |
| | Formula wo/Space-Saver spare | 85.00 |
| | Formula w/Space-Saver spare | 68.00 |
| | Trans Am wo/Space-Saver spare | 45.00 |
| | Trans Am w/Space-Saver spare | 36.00 |
| 39W/QBW | FR78x15 whitewall steel-belted radial tires | |
| | (base, Esprit, Formula) | |
| | Wo/Space-Saver spare | 33.00 |
| | W/Space-Saver spare | 26.40 |
| 39Y/QFM | F78x14 whitewall fiberglass tires | |
| | (base, Esprit) | |
| | Wo/Space-Saver spare (credit) | (73.00) |
| | W/Space-Saver spare | (60.40) |
| 39Z/QFL | F78x14 blackwall fiberglass tires | |
| | (base, Esprit) | |
| | Wo/Space-Saver spare | (106.00) |
| | W/Space-Saver spare | (66.00) |
| 381/G80 | Safe-T-Track differential axle | |
| | V87 | NC |
| | S87, T87, U87 | 49.00 |
| 401/U63 | AM radio | 69.00 |
| 403/U69 | AM/FM radio | 135.00 |
| 405/U58 | AM/FM stereo radio | 233.00 |
| 411/U80 | Rear seat speaker | 19.00 |

| | | |
|---|---|---:|
| 412/U57 | 8 track stereo player | 130.00 |
| 414/C24 | Recessed wipers (S87, U87) | 18.00 |
| 422/D35 | Sport mirrors; LH remote control, RH fixed | |
| | S87 | 27.00 |
| | T87, U87, V87 | NC |
| 424/D58 | Rear seat console | 41.00 |
| 431/D55 | Front seat console | 68.00 |
| 432/D34 | RH visor vanity mirror | 3.00 |
| 441/AK1 | Custom seatbelts & Soft-Tone warning | 19.00 |
| 444/T63 | Headlamp warning buzzer | 6.00 |
| 461/D80 | Custom cushion steering wheel | |
| | (S87 only) | 16.00 |
| 464/NK3 | Formula steering wheel | |
| | S87 | 57.00 |
| | Std w/V87, T87, U87 | 41.00 |
| 471/P06 | Wheel trim rings | |
| | (S87, U87, wo/474/N98) | 30.00 |
| 472/P02 | Custom finned wheel covers | |
| | S87, U87 | 54.00 |
| | T87 | 24.00 |
| 474/N98 | Rally II wheels & trim rings (NC on V87) | |
| | S87, U87, wo/684/N65 | 91.00 |
| | S87, U87, w/684/N65 | 78.80 |
| | T87, wo/684/N65 | 61.00 |
| | T87 w/684/N65 | 48.80 |
| 476/P01 | Deluxe wheel covers (NC w/T87, | |
| | S87, U87) | 30.00 |
| 478/P05 | Honeycomb wheels (NC w/V87) | |
| | S87, U87 wo/684/N65 | 127.00 |
| | S87, U87 w/684/N65 | 107.60 |
| | T87 wo/684/N65 | 97.00 |
| | T87 w/684/N65 | 77.60 |
| 481/B80 | Roof drip moldings | |
| | Std w/T87, wo/Cordova vinyl trim | 15.00 |
| | W/Cordova vinyl top | NC |
| 484/B85 | Windowsill & rear hood edge molding | |
| | (std w/T87) | 21.00 |
| 491/B96 | Wheel lip moldings (S87, U87; std w/T87; | |
| | NA w/V87) | 16.00 |
| 492/B93 | Door edge guards | 7.00 |
| 494/B84 | Bodyside moldings (exc V87) | 35.00 |
| 502/JL2 | Front power disc brakes | |
| | (std w/U87, V87) | 55.00 |
| 504/N33 | Tilt steering wheel | 49.00 |
| 511/JL1 | Pedal Trim Package (std w/T87, Y90) | 5.00 |
| 512/WW7 | Trans Am hood decal (V87 only) | 55.00 |
| 541/VJ9 | Calif emissions equipment & test | 45.00 |
| 551/A31 | Power windows | 91.00 |
| 554/AU3 | Power door locks | 56.00 |
| 571/AQ1 | Soft-Ray glass, all windows | 43.00 |
| 572/AQ2 | Soft-Ray glass, windshield only | 34.00 |
| 582/C60 | Custom AC | 435.00 |

| | | |
|---|---|---|
| 584/BS1 | Added acoustical insulation | |
| | (std in T87) | 20.00 |
| 591/UA1 | HD battery | 11.00 |
| 592/C49 | Electric rear window defroster | 70.00 |
| 594/C50 | Rear window defogger | 41.00 |
| 601/K05 | Engine block heater | 11.00 |
| 602/K45 | HD air cleaner (std w/Trans Am) | 11.00 |
| 622/B32 | Front floor mats | 8.00 |
| 638/D98 | Accent stripes (exc V87) | 43.00 |
| 654/Y92 | Lamp Group (glovebox, instrument panel | |
| | courtesy, luggage) | 11.50 |
| 681/D80 | Rear air spoiler (NA T87; std w/V87) | 45.00 |
| 684/N65 | Space-Saver spare tire | NC |
| 704/UR1 | Fuel economy vacuum gauge (exc V87) | 22.50 |
| 711/U35 | Electric clock | |
| | Wo/Rally gauges or speedometer | |
| | & clock | 16.00 |
| | W/Rally gauges or speedometer & clock | NC |
| 712/W63 | Rally gauges & clock (S87, T87, U87) | 50.00 |
| 714/WW8 | Rally cluster w/clock & tachometer | |
| | (NC w/V87) | 99.00 |
| 804/U18 | Speedometer w/km & clock | 21.00 |
| PVT/C09 | Cordova vinyl top | 99.00 |
| —/L75 | 455 ci V-8 4V engine (V87) | 150.00 |

## Facts

The Firebird got a new wraparound rear window, and the front grille housed lamps at the outside ends of its opening. The grille also used horizontal slats replacing the vertical slats of 1974.

All Firebirds got the RTS suspension system and 15 in. wheels. Standard tires were FR78x15, with the Trans Am getting GR70x15s.

All Firebirds got catalytic converters and single exhaust systems. The higher-output engines simulated dual exhausts by having twin outlets. HEI ignition was standard on all engines.

Engine availability was unchanged on the base and Esprit. The Formula was limited to the 350 and 400 ci V-8 four-barrels, and the Trans Am was available only with the 400 ci V-8.

The 455 ci V-8 returned as a midyear introduction. Labeled the 455 HO, it came with a four-barrel carburetor, a single exhaust with dual outlets, a four-speed manual transmission, a 3.23:1 rear axle ratio and a 200 hp rating. It was not available on California-bound Formulas or Trans Ams.

The Firebird's speedometer now read in kilometers as well as miles per hour. Top speed indicated was 100 mph, or 160 kmph. A fuel economy gauge became part of the W63 Rally gauge option. However, the Rally cluster with clock and tachometer, option WW8, was still available.

The accent side stripe came in a three-color combination, depending on exterior body color. The alternatives were light orange, dark orange and black; light blue, bright blue and black; and yellow, dark green and black.

Trans Am color choices expanded with the addition of Sterling Silver. Stellar Blue replaced Admiralty Blue, being the only other color change.

Three wheels were available on the Trans Am: the honeycomb, the Rally II and the Rally IIs painted to match the car's body color.

All Firebird automatic transmissions were the M38 Turbo Hydra-matic TH350. The larger, stronger TH400 previously mated with the 400 and 455 engines would not fit with the necessary catalytic converter.

*1975 Firebird Formula 400*

# Chapter 10

# 1976 Firebird

## Production

| Model | Manual | Automatic | Total |
|---|---|---|---|
| 2 dr base 6 & 8 cyl | | | 21,206 |
| 2 dr Esprit 6 & 8 cyl | | | 22,252 |
| 2 dr Formula 8 cyl | | | 20,613 |
| 2 dr Trans Am w/400 ci 8 cyl | | | 37,015 |
| 2 dr Trans Am w/455 ci 8 cyl | 7,099 | — | 7,099 |
| 2 dr Trans Am w/400 ci 8 cyl* | | | 1,628 |
| 2 dr Trans Am w/455 ci 8 cyl* | 319 | — | 319 |
| 2 dr Trans Am w/400 ci 8 cyl† | | | 533 |
| 2 dr Trans Am w/455 ci 8 cyl† | 110 | — | 110 |
| Total | | | 110,775 |

*Limited Edition coupe.
†Limited Edition T-top coupe.

## Serial Numbers

**Description**
2S87W6N100001
2—Pontiac
S—Firebird body series (S = base, T = Esprit, U = Formula,
   V = Trans Am)
87—body style (87 = 2 dr coupe)
W—engine code
6—last digit of model year (6 = 1976)
N—assembly plant (N = Norwood)
100001—consecutive sequence number

**Location**
   On plate attached to left side of dash, visible through windshield.

## Engine VIN Codes
D—250 ci
H, J, M, P—350 ci
N, Z—400 ci
W—455 ci

## Engine Identification Codes
YB, YR—350 ci V-8 2 bbl 160 hp automatic
ZF, ZX—350 ci V-8 4 bbl 165 hp automatic
WT—400 ci V-8 4 bbl 185 hp manual
YS, YZ—400 ci V-8 4 bbl 185 hp automatic
ZK—400 ci V-8 4 bbl 185 hp automatic Calif
WX—455 ci V-8 4 bbl 200 hp manual

## Carburetors
350 ci 160 hp—17056161, 17056163, 17056171
350 ci 165 hp—17056658, 17056564
400 ci 185 hp manual—17056263
400 ci 185 hp automatic—17056264
400 ci 185 hp automatic—17056564 Calif
455 ci 200 hp manual—17056261

## Head Castings
350, 400, 455 ci—6X or 6S

## Exterior Color Codes

| | | | |
|---|---|---|---|
| Cameo White | 11 | Metalime Green | 40 |
| Sterling Silver | 13 | Alpine Green | 49 |
| Starlight Black | 19 | Bavarian Cream | 50 |
| Athena Blue | 28 | Goldenrod Yellow | 51 |
| Polaris Blue | 35 | Buckskin Tan | 65 |
| Firethorn Red | 36 | Durango Bronze | 67 |
| Cordovan Maroon | 37 | Carousel Red | 78 |

## Interior Trim Codes

| Color | Vinyl Buckets | Custom Buckets |
|---|---|---|
| White | 11M1 | — |
| Buckskin | 64M1 | — |
| Black | 19M1 | — |
| Blue | 26N1 | — |
| Firethorn | 71N1 | — |
| Firethorn/White seats | 91V1 | — |
| Blue/White seats | 92N1 | — |
| Black/White seats | 97N1 | — |
| White/Blue trim | 11M1/341 | 11N1/341 |
| White/Firethorn trim | 11M1/343 | 11N1/343 |
| White/Lime trim | 11M1/344 | 11N1/344 |

## Vinyl Top Color Codes

| | | | | |
|---|---|---|---|---|
| White | 1 | Green | | 5 |
| Black | 2 | Blue | | 7 |
| Sandstone | 3 | Red | | |
| Cordovan | | Silver | | |
| Burgundy | | | | |

## Options

| Sales Code/UPC | Description | Retail Price |
|---|---|---|
| | 2 dr coupe | $3,906.00 |
| | 2 dr coupe Esprit | 4,162.00 |
| | 2 dr coupe Formula | 4,566.00 |
| | 2 dr coupe Trans Am | 4,987.00 |
| 32N/Y90 | Custom Trim Group | |
| | (U87, W87 only; std w/T87) | 81.00 |
| 37D/L22 | 250 ci L-6 1V engine (S87, T87) | NC |

| Sales Code/UPC | Description | Retail Price |
|---|---|---|
| 37E/L76 | 350 ci V–8 4V engine (Calif only) | |
| | S87, T87 (required w/Turbo | |
| | Hydra-matic) | 195.00 |
| | U87 | 55.00 |
| 37M/L30 | 350 ci V–8 2V engine (S87, T87; | |
| | NA Calif; std w/U87; required | |
| | w/Turbo Hydra-matic) | 140.00 |
| 37S/L78 | 400 ci V–8 4V engine (NA Calif) | |
| | S87, T87; required w/Turbo | |
| | Hydra-matic, 38F/M21 | 258.00 |
| | U87; requires Turbo Hydra-matic, | |
| | 38F/M21; std w/W87 | 118.00 |
| 37W/L75 | 455 ci V–8 4V engine (W87 only; NA Calif; | |
| | required w/Turbo Hydra-matic, | |
| | 38F/M21) | 125.00 |
| 38B/M15 | 3 speed manual transmission (incl | |
| | floor shift; w/37D/L22 only) | NC |
| 38F/M21 | Close-ratio 4 speed manual transmission | |
| | (NA Calif) | |
| | W/37S/L78, 37W/L75 only | 242.00 |
| | In W87 | NC |
| 38L/M40 | Turbo Hydra-matic transmission | |
| | (S87, T87; std w/U87, W87) | 262.00 |
| 40B/QBU | FR78x15 black-belted radial tires | |
| | (S87, T87, U87) | NC |
| 40C/QFL | F78x14 blackwall fiberglass radial tires | |
| | (S87, T87) | |
| | Wo/441/N65 | (97.45) |
| | W/441/N65 | (77.96) |
| 40D/QFM | F78x14 whitewall fiberglass radial tires | |
| | (S87, T87) | |
| | Wo/441/N65 | (62.45) |
| | W/441/N65 | (49.96) |
| 40F/QCY | GR70x15 white-letter steel-belted radial | |
| | tires (required w/441/N65) | |
| | U87 | 72.84 |
| | W87 | 38.40 |
| 40G/QBX | GR70x15 blackwall steel-belted radial tires | |
| | (U87; std w/W87) | 34.44 |
| 40L/QBP | FR78x15 white-letter steel-belted radial | |
| | tires (exc W87) | |
| | Wo/441/N65 | 46.00 |
| | W/441/N65 | 36.80 |
| 40W/QBW | FR78x15 whitewall steel-belted radial tires | |
| | (exc W87) | |
| | Wo/441/N65 | 35.00 |
| | W/441/N65 | 28.00 |
| 358/D98 | Vinyl accent stripes (S87, T87, U87) | 46.00 |
| 391/G80 | Safe-T-Track axle (S87, T87, U87; | |
| | std w/W87) | 51.00 |

| | | |
|---|---|---:|
| 411/U63 | AM radio | 75.00 |
| 413/U69 | AM/FM radio | 137.00 |
| 415/U58 | AM/FM stereo radio | 233.00 |
| 421/U80 | Rear seat speaker (opt only w/411/U63, 413/U69) | 20.00 |
| 422/U57 | 8 track stereo player (required w/D55 & radio) | 134.00 |
| 431/A31 | Power windows (w/581/D55 only) | 99.00 |
| 434/AU3 | Power door locks | 62.00 |
| 441/N65 | Stowaway spare tire (S87, T87, U87; std w/W87) | (1.22) |
| 442/A01 | Soft-Ray tinted glass, all windows | 46.00 |
| 444/U57 | Tilt steering wheel | 52.00 |
| 452/JL2 | Power front disc brakes (required w/V-8; std w/U87, W87) | 58.00 |
| 461/C49 | Electric rear window defroster (V-8s only) | 77.00 |
| 462/C50 | Rear window defogger | 48.00 |
| 474/U35 | Electric clock (NC w/502/W63, 504/WW8) | 18.00 |
| 481/UR1 | Vacuum gauge (S87, T87, U87 w/502/W63 only) | 25.00 |
| 492/C60 | Custom AC | 452.00 |
| 502/W63 | Rally gauge cluster & clock (S87, T87, U87; required w/481/UR1 w/6 cyl) | 54.00 |
| 504/WW8 | Rally gauge cluster w/clock & tachometer (S87, T87, U87; V-8 only) | 106.00 |
| 521/BS1 | Added acoustical insulation (std w/Esprit) | 25.00 |
| 524/AK1 | Custom front & rear seatbelts & front shoulder strap | 20.00 |
| 541/N30 | Custom cushion steering wheel (S87; std w/T87, U87) | 17.00 |
| 544/NK3 | Formula steering wheel (NC w/W87) | |
| | S87 | 60.00 |
| | T87, U87 | 43.00 |
| 554/N98 | Argent silver Rally II wheels & trim rings | |
| | 5 w/ fiberglass tires wo/441/N65 on S87 | 113.00 |
| | 4 w/fiberglass tires w/441/N65 on S87 | 97.00 |
| | 4 wo/fiberglass tires on S87 | 97.00 |
| | 5 w/fiberglass tires wo/441/N65 on T87 | 81.00 |
| | 4 w/fiberglass tires w/441/N65 on T87 | 65.00 |
| | 4 wo/fiberglass tires on T87 | 65.00 |
| | 4 wo/fiberglass tires on U87 | 97.00 |
| | 4 wo/fiberglass tires on W87 | NC |
| 556/P01 | Deluxe wheel covers (S87, U87; NC w/T87; NA w/W87) | 6.00 |

| Sales Code/UPC | Description | Retail Price |
|---|---|---|
| 558/P05 | 4 honeycomb wheels w/radial tires | |
| | S87, U87 | 135.00 |
| | T87; NC w/W87 | 103.00 |
| 559/N67 | Body-color Rally II wheels & trim rings | |
| | 5 w/fiberglass tires wo/441/N65 on S87 | 113.00 |
| | 4 w/fiberglass tires w/441/N65 on S87 | 97.00 |
| | 4 wo/fiberglass tires on S87 | 97.00 |
| | 5 w/fiberglass tires wo/441/N65 on T87 | 81.00 |
| | 4 w/fiberglass tires w/441/N65 on T87 | 65.00 |
| | 4 wo/fiberglass tires on T87 | 65.00 |
| | 4 wo/fiberglass tires on U87 | 97.00 |
| | 4 wo/fiberglass tires on W87 | NC |
| 561/JL1 | Pedal Trim Package (S87, U87, W87 wo/Y90; std w/T87) | 6.00 |
| 562/D80 | Rear air spoiler (S87, T87, U87; std w/W87) | 48.00 |
| 572/D58 | Rear seat console | 43.00 |
| 574/C24 | Recessed windshield wipers (S87, T87; std w/U87, W87) | 22.00 |
| 581/D55 | Front console (required w/Turbo Hydra-matic; std w/U87) | 71.00 |
| 582/W50 | Formula Appearance Package (colors 11, 78, 51, 13, N, T, V only) | 100.00 |
| 584/B80 | Roof drip moldings (S87, U87 wo/CVT/CB7; W87; std w/T87, CVT/CB7) | 16.00 |
| 591/B85 | Window & rear hood moldings (S87, U87, W87; std w/T87) | 22.00 |
| 601/B32 | Front floor mats | 8.00 |
| 602/B33 | Rear floor mats | 7.00 |
| 611/B84 | Color-keyed vinyl body moldings (S87, T87, U87) | 38.00 |
| 612/B93 | Door edge guards | 8.00 |
| 614/B96 | Wheel lip moldings (S87, U87; std w/T87; NA w/W87) | 17.00 |
| 631/Y92 | Lamp Group (glovebox, instrument panel courtesy, luggage compartment) | 14.00 |
| 642/D35 | Dual sport OSRV mirrors, LH remote control (std w/T87, U87, W87) | 29.00 |
| 652/D34 | Visor vanity mirror | 4.00 |
| 664/WW7 | Hood decal (W87 only) | 58.00 |
| 674/K97 | HD alternator (V-8s only) | |
| | Wo/462/C50, w/492/C60 | 42.00 |
| | W/462/C50, 492/C60 | NC |
| 681/UA1 | HD battery | 16.00 |
| 682/VQ2 | Supercooling radiator (wo/492/C60; $22 less w/492/C60) | 49.00 |

| | | |
|---|---|---|
| 684/K05 | Engine block heater | 12.00 |
| 721/VJ9 | Calif emissions equipment & test | 50.00 |
| 802/UN9 | Radio Accommodation Package (NC w/opt radios) | 22.00 |
| CVT/CB7 | Canopy top (S87, T87, U87; NA w/W87) | 96.00 |

## Facts

The 1976 Firebird's front end was restyled. Most noticeable in the front was the redesigned bumper, which had twin air inlets and also housed the turn signal lamps. The grille got a hexagonal mesh. In the rear, the black bumper strip was removed, giving the rear a cleaner look. Cars with the simulated dual exhaust systems got the side-splitter extensions.

Both the standard and the custom interiors were redesigned. A rosewood appliqué replaced the African crossfire mahogany on the dash.

The Formula Firebird got a new optional appearance package, W50. It consisted of yellow body paint and black lower body paint with large Formula lettering on the bottoms of both doors. The yellow and black areas were separated by red striping. The grille was also blacked out and the hood scoops were trimmed with red striping. A red Formula decal was located above the left grille opening next to the headlight. As the yellow-black scheme gained popularity, other combinations were added.

The Formula's performance hood was redesigned. No longer a fiberglass unit, it sported redesigned, sunken simulated scoops. The Formula also came with a front console as standard equipment.

Engine availability was the same, although certain engine-transmission combinations were not available in California. As the 350 ci two-barrel engine was not certified for California, the 350 ci four-barrel engine was optional on the base and Esprit and only with the automatic transmission. The standard engine on the Formula was the 350 ci V–8 two-barrel, except in California where the 350 ci four-barrel teamed to the Turbo hydra-matic. The 400 ci V–8 was standard on the Trans Am and optional on the Formula; however, California-bound cars again came only with the auto-matic. The 455 HO was available only on the Trans Am except in California, as it came with the four-speed manual.

This would be the last year for the 455 ci engine and the honeycomb wheels.

Trans Ams were available in Cameo White, Sterling Silver, Firethorn Red, Goldenrod Yellow and Carousel Red.

A black-and-gold Trans Am Limited Edition was issued to commemorate Pontiac's fiftieth anniversary. All examples were supposed to get removable T-tops, but problems with the Hurst tops limited production of T-top equipped cars (Y82) to 643. All 1976 Limited Editions were painted black with gold striping and received a gold Trans Am hood decal, gold grilles, gold headlight bezels, gold polycast honeycomb wheels, gold interior appliqués, a gold steering wheel, gold Trans Am decals and a special gold fiftieth-anniversary decal affixed below the Trans Am fender decals. Both 400 ci and 455 ci engines were available on the Limited Edition.

Originally stated to get black chrome side-splitter exhausts, the Limited Edition usually ended up getting the stock chrome units, though a few cars got the black ones.

*1976 Firebird Formula*

# Chapter 11

# 1977 Firebird

## Production

| Model | Manual | Automatic | Total |
|---|---|---|---|
| 2 dr base 6 & 8 cyl | | | 30,642 |
| 2 dr Esprit 6 & 8 cyl | | | 34,548 |
| 2 dr Formula 8 cyl | | | 21,801 |
| 2 dr Trans Am w/400 ci 8 cyl (L78) | — | 29,313 | 29,313 |
| 2 dr Trans Am w/400 ci 8 cyl (W72) | 8,319 | 10,466 | 18,785 |
| 2 dr Trans Am w/403 ci 8 cyl (L80) | — | 5,079 | 5,079 |
| 2 dr Trans Am w/400 ci 8 cyl* (L78) | — | 748 | 748 |
| 2 dr Trans Am w/400 ci 8 cyl* (W72) | 384 | 549 | 933 |
| 2 dr Trans Am w/403 ci 8 cyl* (L80) | — | 180 | 180 |
| 2 dr Trans Am w/400 ci 8 cyl† (L78) | — | 6,030 | 6,030 |
| 2 dr Trans Am w/400 ci 8 cyl† (W72) | 2,699 | 3,760 | 6,459 |
| 2 dr Trans Am w/403 ci 8 cyl† (L80) | — | 1,217 | 1,217 |
| Total | | | 155,735 |

*Special Edition coupe.
†Special Edition T-top coupe.

## Serial Numbers

**Description**
2W87Z7N100001
2—Pontiac
W—Firebird body series (S = base, T = Esprit, U = Formula, W = Trans Am)
87—body style (87 = 2 dr coupe)
Z—engine code
7—last digit of model year (7 = 1977)
N—assembly plant (N = Norwood)
100001—consecutive sequence number

**Location**
On plate attached to left side of dash, visible through windshield.

## Engine VIN Codes

C—231 ci Buick
Y—301 ci
L, R—350 ci

X—350 ci Oldsmobile
Z—400 ci
K—403 ci Oldsmobile

## Engine Identification Codes

SG, SI, SK, SM, ST, SU—231 ci V-6 2 bbl 105 hp manual or automatic
WB—301 ci V-8 2 bbl 135 hp manual
YH, YK—301 ci V-8 2 bbl 135 hp automatic
Y9—350 ci V-8 4 bbl 170 hp automatic
XA—400 ci V-8 4 bbl 180 hp automatic
WA—400 ci V-8 4 bbl 200 hp manual
Y6—400 ci V-8 4 bbl 200 hp automatic
U2, U3, VA, VB—403 ci V-8 4 bbl 185 hp automatic

### Carburetors

301 ci manual—17057173
301 ci automatic—17057172
350 ci 170 hp—17057262
400 ci 180 hp—17057264
400 ci 200 hp manual—17057263
400 ci 200 hp automatic—17057266

## Head Castings

301 ci—01
350, 400 ci—6X

## Exterior Color Codes

| | | | |
|---|---|---|---|
| Cameo White | 11 | Goldenrod Yellow | 51 |
| Sterling Silver | 13 | Gold Metallic | 55 |
| Starlight Black | 19 | Bright Blue | 58 |
| Lombard Blue | 21 | Mojave Tan | 61 |
| Glacier Blue | 22 | Buckskin Metallic | 63 |
| Nautilus Blue | 29 | Brentwood Brown | 69 |
| Firethorn Red | 36 | Buccaneer Red | 75 |
| Aquamarine | 38 | Mandarin Orange | 78 |
| Bahia Green | 44 | | |

## Standard Interior Trim Codes

| Color | Vinyl Buckets | Custom Buckets |
|---|---|---|
| White | 11R1 | 11N1 |
| Black | 19R1 | 19N1 |
| Blue | — | 24N1 |
| Buckskin | 64R1 | 64N1 |
| Firethorn | 71R1 | 71N1 |
| Blue/White seats | — | 92N1 |
| Firethorn/White seats | 97R1 | 97N1 |
| White/Blue trim | 11R1/26X | 11N1/26X |
| White/Turquoise trim | 11R1/34X | 11N1/34X |
| White/Saddle trim | 11R1/64X | 11N1/64X |

| | | | |
|---|---|---|---|
| White/Firethorn trim | 11R1/71X | 11N1/71X |
| Black cloth | — | 19B1 |
| Blue cloth | — | 24B1 |
| Firethorn cloth | — | 71B1 |

## Vinyl Top Color Codes

| | | | |
|---|---|---|---|
| White | 11 | Green | 44 |
| Silver | 13 | Buckskin | 61 |
| Black | 19 | | |
| Blue | 22 | | |
| Firethorn | 36 | | |

## Options

| UPC | Description | Retail Price |
|---|---|---|
| | 2 dr coupe | $4,270.00 |
| | 2 dr coupe Esprit | 4,551.00 |
| | 2 dr coupe Formula | 4,977.00 |
| | 2 dr coupe Trans Am | 5,456.00 |
| AK1 | Custom belts (std in T87 w/W60) | 21.00 |
| AU3 | Power door locks | 68.00 |
| A01 | Tinted glass, all windows | 50.00 |
| A31 | Power windows (required w/D55) | 108.00 |
| A90 | Remote control deck lid release | 18.00 |
| BS1 | Added acoustical insulation (std w/T87) | 27.00 |
| B37 | Color-keyed front & rear floor mats | 18.00 |
| B80 | Roof drip moldings | |
| | Std w/T87; S87, U87 wo/CB7 | 17.00 |
| | W87 | 17.00 |
| B84 | Vinyl bodyside moldings | 40.00 |
| B85 | Windowsill & rear hood moldings (std w/T87) | 24.00 |
| B93 | Door edge guard moldings | 9.00 |
| B96 | Wheel opening moldings | |
| | S87 | 18.00 |
| | U87 wo/W50 | 18.00 |
| CB7 | Canopy top (NA w/W87) | 105.00 |
| CC1 | Glass sunroof w/dual hatches (wo/Y82) | 587.00 |
| C49 | Electric rear window defroster | 82.00 |
| C60 | AC | 478.00 |
| C95 | Dome reading lamp | 16.00 |
| D34 | Visor vanity mirror | 4.00 |
| D35 | Dual sport outside mirrors, LH remote control | 31.00 |
| D55 | Front console (required w/M40; S87, T87) | 75.00 |
| D58 | Rear console | 46.00 |
| D64 | Illuminated visor vanity mirror | 32.00 |
| D80 | Rear spoiler (S87, T87; std w/U87, W87) | 51.00 |
| D98 | Vinyl accent strips (all exc W87) | 49.00 |
| G80 | Safe-T-Track differential (std w/W87) | 54.00 |
| JL1 | Pedal trim packages | |
| | S87 | 6.00 |
| | U87, W87; wo/Y90 | 6.00 |

| UPC | Description | Retail Price |
|---|---|---|
| JL2 | Power brakes (required w/all V-8s; S87, T87) | 61.00 |
| K05 | Engine block heater | 13.00 |
| K30 | Cruise control | 80.00 |
| LD | 231 ci V-6 2V engine (S87, T87) | Std |
| L27 | 301 ci V-8 2V engine (required w/M20, M40; S87, T87) | 65.00 |
| L34 | 350 ci V-8 4V engine | |
| | S87, T87 | 155.00 |
| | U87 | 90.00 |
| L76 | 350 ci V-8 4V engine (Calif only) | |
| | S87, T87 | 155.00 |
| | U87 | 90.00 |
| L78 | 400 ci V-8 4V engine (required w/M40; U87) | 155.00 |
| L80 | 403 ci V-8 4V engine (U87) | 155.00 |
| M20 | 4 speed manual transmission (L27, W72 only; (S87, T87) | 257.00 |
| M40 | Turbo Hydra-matic automatic transmission (S87, T87) | 282.00 |
| NA6 | High-altitude performance option | 22.00 |
| NK3 | Formula steering wheel | |
| | S87 | 61.00 |
| | T87, U87 | 43.00 |
| N30 | Luxury cushion steering wheel (S87) | 18.00 |
| N33 | Tilt steering wheel | 57.00 |
| N65 | Stowaway spare tire | NC |
| N67 | Body-color Rally II wheels w/trim rings | |
| | S87, U87 | 106.00 |
| | T87 | 72.00 |
| N95 | Wire wheel covers | |
| | NA w/W87; S87, U87 | 134.00 |
| | T87 | 100.00 |
| N98 | Argent silver Rally II wheels w/trim rings | |
| | S87, U87 | 106.00 |
| | T87 | 72.00 |
| OBP | FR8-15 white-letter steel-belted radial tires (exc W87) | |
| | Wo/N65 | 55.00 |
| | W/N65 | 44.00 |
| OBW | FR78-15 whitewall steel-belted radial tires (exc W87) | |
| | Wo/N65 | 41.00 |
| | W/N65 | 33.00 |
| OKM | FR78-15 blackwall fiber-belted radial tires (S87, T87) | |
| | Wo/N65 | (45.00) |
| | W/N65 | (36.00) |
| OKN | FR78-15 whitewall fiber-belted radial tires (S87, T87) | |
| | Wo/N65 | (4.00) |
| | W/N65 | (3.00) |
| P01 | Deluxe wheel covers (NC T87; S87, U87) | 34.00 |

| | | |
|---|---|---:|
| QBX | Rally RTS Handling Package (required w/N65; | |
| | U87 only) | 70.00 |
| QCY | Rally RTS Package | |
| | U87 | 116.00 |
| | W87 | 46.00 |
| UA1 | HD maintenance-free battery | 31.00 |
| UN8 | 23 channel CB radio (required w/D55, UN9) | 195.00 |
| UN9 | Radio Accommodation Package | |
| | (NC w/opt radio) | 23.00 |
| UR1 | Economy & vacuum gauges | |
| | (together w/W63 only; exc W87) | 27.00 |
| U35 | Electric clock (NC w/Rally gauges) | 21.00 |
| U57 | 8 track stereo player (required w/D55, | |
| | opt radio) | 134.00 |
| U58 | AM/FM stereo | 233.00 |
| U63 | AM radio | 79.00 |
| U69 | AM/FM radio | 137.00 |
| U80 | Rear speaker (w/AM, AM/FM radio only) | 23.00 |
| VJ9 | Calif emissions equipment | 70.00 |
| V02 | Supercooling radiator | |
| | Wo/C60, V81 | 53.00 |
| | W/C60; wo/V81 | 29.00 |
| | W/V81 | NC |
| V81 | Light Trailer Group | |
| | Wo/C60 | 64.00 |
| | W/C60 | 40.00 |
| WW7 | Trans Am hood decal (W87 only) | 62.00 |
| WW8 | Rally gauges w/clock & tachometer | |
| | (w/V-8 only; exc W87) | 116.00 |
| W50 | Formula Appearance Package (U87 only) | 127.00 |
| W60 | Sky Bird Appearance Package (T87) | |
| | W/Lombardy trim | 342.00 |
| | W/doeskin trim | 315.00 |
| W63 | Rally gauges & clock (required w/UR1 w/LD; | |
| | exc W87) | 27.00 |
| W72 | 400 ci V-8 4V engine (required w/M20, M40) | |
| | U87 | 205.00 |
| | W87 | 50.00 |
| YJ8 | Cast-aluminum snowflake wheels | |
| | S87 | 227.00 |
| | T87 wo/W60 | 193.00 |
| | U87 | 227.00 |
| | W87 | 121.00 |
| Y81 | W87 Special Edition Package wo/T-top | 556.00 |
| Y82 | W87 Special Edition Package w/T-top | 1,143.00 |
| Y90 | Custom trim | |
| | Vinyl doeskin; U87, W87 | 91.00 |
| | Lombardy cloth; U87, W87 | 118.00 |
| | Regular vinyl; T87 wo/W60 | 27.00 |
| Y92 | Lamp Group Package | 16.00 |
| Y96 | Firm Ride Package (NC w/V81) | 11.00 |

## Facts

The 1977 Firebird got dual rectangular headlights in a new grille. The hood was also redesigned with a wider hood bulge area. The Formula's hood was redone with a different hood scoop design.

Three engines from Pontiac were complemented with three engines from other GM divisions. The standard six-cylinder engine, which had been the Chevrolet inline six, was replaced by the Buick V-6 on the base and Esprit models. Optional on these models was a new Pontiac V-8 displacing 301 ci and rated at 135 hp. Based on the Pontiac V-8, the 301 weighed 119 lb less than the 350 ci V-8 because of its thin-wall castings. The 301 weighed in at 452 lb. The only other optional engine on the base and Esprit was the Pontiac 350 ci two-barrel or the Oldsmobile 350 ci V-8. The Oldsmobile V-8 came on high-altitude and California Firebirds. Only with the 301 ci V-8 was a four-speed manual transmission available.

The standard engine on the Formula was the Pontiac 301 ci V-8. Optional were the two 350 ci V-8s, with the Oldsmobile version relegated to California and high-altitude duty. Also optional were the two Pontiac 400s and the L80 Oldsmobile 403 ci V-8. The Oldsmobile V-8 was available only for California and high-altitude cars.

The Trans Am came only with the L78 Pontiac 400 ci V-8 or the W72 400 ci 200 hp V-8. The Oldsmobile 403 ci V-8 was the only engine available on California and high-altitude Trans Ams mated to the TH350 automatic transmission.

The W72 was the only 400 ci V-8 that could be had with the manual four-speed transmission.

The L78 and Oldsmobile 403 ci equipped Trans Ams came with 6.6 liter identification on the shaker hood scoop; the more powerful W72 got T/A 6.6 decals.

The Esprit was available with the Sky Bird Appearance Package, W60. It came with two-tone blue paint, canopy stripes, blue painted grille liners and taillight bezels, and blue cast-aluminum snowflake wheels. In the interior, a blue Formula steering wheel was used.

The Formula could still be had with the Formula Appearance Package, W50. Similar to the package offered in 1976, it had color choices expanded to six: Cameo White/black with blue striping, Sterling Silver/charcoal and light red, Black/gold, Goldenrod Yellow/gold, orange and black, Glacier Blue/light and medium blue and black, and Buccaneer Red/light and dark red and black.

The Trans Am's rear spoiler was standard on the Formula.

Replacing the honeycomb wheels were the cast-aluminum snowflake wheels, made in 14 and 15 in. sizes. The 15x7 in. wheels were optional on the Trans Am in either natural or body-color versions. The Rally IIs were standard. All wheels got the same GR70x15 radial tires.

Trans Am exterior colors were Cameo White, Sterling Silver, Starlight Black, Goldenrod Yellow, Brentwood Brown and Buccaneer Red.

The 1976 Limited Edition color scheme and T-tops were carried over for 1977; however, the model was called the Trans Am Special Edition. The T-tops, built by Hurst, were coded CC1.

*1977 Firebird Formula*

# Chapter 12

# 1978 Firebird

## Production

| Model | Manual | Automatic | Total |
|---|---|---|---|
| 2 dr base 6 & 8 cyl | | | 32,671 |
| 2 dr Esprit 6 & 8 cyl | | | 36,926 |
| 2 dr Formula 8 cyl | | . | 24,346 |
| 2 dr Trans Am w/400 ci 8 cyl (L78) | 6,777 | 57,035 | 63,812 |
| 2 dr Trans Am w/400 ci 8 cyl (W72) | 4,112 | 4,139 | 8,251 |
| 2 dr Trans Am w/403 ci 8 cyl (L80) | — | 8,969 | 8,969 |
| 2 dr Trans Am w/400 ci 8 cyl* (L78) | 489 | 2,856 | 3,345 |
| 2 dr Trans Am w/400 ci 8 cyl† (L78) | 20 | 68 | 88 |
| 2 dr Trans Am w/403 ci 8 cyl† (L80) | — | 210 | 210 |
| 2 dr Trans Am w/400 ci 8 cyl‡ (L78) | 1,267 | 6,529 | 7,796 |
| 2 dr Trans Am w/400 ci 8 cyl‡ (L80) | — | 880 | 880 |
| Total | | | 187,294 |

*Black Special Edition built at Norwood plant.
†Black Special Edition built at Van Nuys plant.
‡Gold Special Edition.

## Serial Numbers

**Description**
2W87Z8N100001
2—Pontiac
W—Firebird body series (S = base, T = Esprit, U = Formula, W = Trans Am)
87—body style (87 = 2 dr coupe)
Z—engine code
8—last digit of model year (8 = 1978)
N—assembly plant (N = Norwood, L = Van Nuys)
100001—consecutive sequence number

**Location**
On plate attached to left side of dash, visible through windshield.

## Engine VIN Codes

A—3.8 L Buick
U—5.0 L Chevrolet
L—5.7 L Chevrolet
R—5.7 L Oldsmobile
X—5.7 L Buick
Z—6.6 L
K—6.6 L Oldsmobile

## Engine Identification Codes

EA, EC, EE—3.8 L V-6 2 bbl 105 hp manual or automatic
TH, TJ, TK, 3N—5.0 L V-8 2 bbl 135 hp manual or automatic
HF, HJ, HL, HR, 3T—5.7 L V-8 4 bbl 170 hp manual or automatic
YA, YU—6.6 L V-8 4 bbl 180 hp automatic
WC—6.6 L V-8 4 bbl 220 hp manual
X7—6.6 L V-8 4 bbl 220 hp automatic
U2, U3, VA, VB—6.6 L V-8 4 bbl 185 hp automatic

## Pontiac Carburetors

6.6 L 400 ci 180 hp—17058276, 17058278
6.6 L 400 ci 220 hp manual—17058263
6.6 L 400 ci 220 hp automatic—17058266

## Pontiac Head Casting

6.6 L 400 ci—6X

## Exterior Color Codes

| | | | |
|---|---|---|---|
| Cameo White | 11 | Sundance Yellow | 51 |
| Platinum | 15 | Gold Metallic | 55 |
| Starlight Black | 19 | Dark Blue | 58 |
| Glacier Blue | 22 | Laredo Brown | 63 |
| Martinique Blue | 24 | Ember Mist | 67 |
| Lombard Blue | 30 | Chesterfield Brown | 69 |
| Redbird Red | 42 | Medium Red | 72 |
| Berkshire Green | 48 | Mayan Red | 75 |
| Special Edition Gold | 50 | Carmine | 77 |

## Standard Interior Trim Codes

| Color | Vinyl Buckets | Custom Vinyl Buckets | Custom Cloth Buckets |
|---|---|---|---|
| White | 11R1 | 11N1 | — |
| Black | 19R1 | 19N1 | 19B1 |
| Blue | — | 24N1 | 24B1 |
| Camel Tan | 62R1 | 62N1 | 62B1 |
| Carmine | 74R1 | 74N1 | 74B1 |
| White/Blue trim | — | 11N1/24X | — |
| White/Carmine trim | — | 11N1/74X | — |
| White/Ember trim | — | 11N1/67X | — |
| White/Camel Tan trim | — | 11N1/62X | — |

## Vinyl Top Color Codes

| | | | |
|---|---|---|---|
| White | 11 | Black | 19 |
| Silver | 13 | Blue | 22 |

| | | |
|---|---|---|
| Green | 40 | |
| Beige | 61 | |
| Claret | 79 | |

## Options

| UPC | Description | Retail Price |
|---|---|---|
| | 2 dr coupe | $4,593.00 |
| | 2 dr coupe Esprit | 4,897.00 |
| | 2 dr coupe Formula | 5,533.00 |
| | 2 dr coupe Trans Am | 5,889.00 |
| AK1 | Custom belts | |
| | All exec Sky Bird, Red Bird | 20.00 |
| | Sky Bird, Red Bird | NC |
| AU3 | Power door locks | 80.00 |
| AO1 | Tinted glass, all windows | 56.00 |
| A31 | Power windows (required w/D55) | 124.00 |
| A90 | Remote control deck lid release | 21.00 |
| BS1 | Added acoustical insulation | |
| | (NC w/T87) | 29.00 |
| B37 | Color-keyed front & rear floor mats | 21.00 |
| B84 | Roof drip moldings (NA w/WY9, CC1; wo/CB7) | |
| | W/S87, U87 | 20.00 |
| | W/W87 | 20.00 |
| | W/T87 | NC |
| B85 | Windowsill & rear hood moldings (std w/T87) | 25.00 |
| B96 | Wheel opening moldings | |
| | NA w/W87; w/S87; U87; wo/W50 | 21.00 |
| | U87 w/W50; T87 | NC |
| CC1 | Fisher hatch roof | |
| | Wo/Y84, Y88 | 625.00 |
| | W/Y84, Y88 | NC |
| CD4 | Controlled-cycle windshield wipers | 32.00 |
| C49 | Electric rear window defroster | 92.00 |
| C60 | Custom AC | 508.00 |
| CB7 | Canopy top (NA w/W87; incl B80) | 111.00 |
| C95 | Dome reading lamps | 18.00 |
| D34 | Visor vanity mirror | 5.00 |
| D35 | Mirror Group (S87) | 34.00 |
| D55 | Console | |
| | Required w/automatic transmission; S87, T87 | 80.00 |
| | U87, W87 w/automatic transmission | NC |
| D80 | Rear deck spoiler | |
| | S87, T87 | 55.00 |
| | U87, W87 | NC |
| D98 | Vinyl accent stripes (NA w/W87, W50, W60) | 52.00 |
| G80 | Safe-T-Track rear axle (S87, T87, U87) | 60.00 |
| JL2 | Power brakes (required w/V-8 & V-6 w/C60) | |
| | W/S87, T87 | 69.00 |

| | | |
|---|---|---|
| | W/U87, W87 | NC |
| KO5 | Engine block heater | 14.00 |
| K30 | Cruise control (required w/automatic transmission, w/LG3, LM1, L78, W72) | 90.00 |
| K76 | HD 61 amp alternator (available only w/LG3, LM1) | |
| | Wo/C49, C60 | 31.00 |
| | W/C49, C60 | NC |
| K81 | HD 63 amp alternator (available only w/LD5, L78, W72, L80) | |
| | Wo/C49, C60 | 31.00 |
| | W/C49, C60 | NC |
| LD5 | 3.8 L V-6 2V engine (S87, T87; NA w/NA6) | Std |
| LG3 | 5.0 L V-8 2V engine | |
| | S87, T87 | 117.00 |
| | U87 | NC |
| LM1 | 5.7 L V-8 4V engine | |
| | S87, T87 | 265.00 |
| | U87 | 115.00 |
| L78 | 6.6 L V-8 4V engine (NA w/NA6, VJ9; required w/automatic transmission) | |
| | U87 | 205.00 |
| | W87 | NC |
| L80 | 6.6 L 403 ci V-8 4V engine (w/NA6, VJ9 only; required w/automatic transmission) | |
| | U87 | 205.00 |
| | W87 | NC |
| MM3 | 3 speed manual transmission w/floor shift (w/LD5 only) | NC |
| MM4 | 4 speed manual transmission (w/LG3, LM1; NA w/NA6, VJ9) | |
| | U87 | (182.00) |
| | S87, T87 | 125.00 |
| MX1 | 3 speed automatic transmission (required w/D55) | |
| | S87, T87 | 307.00 |
| | U87, W87 | NC |
| M21 | Close-ratio 4 speed manual transmission (w/W72 only; NA w/NA6, VJ9) | |
| | U87 | NC |
| | W87 only | NC |
| NA6 | High-altitude emissions system | 33.00 |
| NK3 | Formula steering wheel | |
| | S87 | 65.00 |
| | T87 wo/W60 | 46.00 |
| | T87 w/W60, W87 | NC |
| | U87 | 46.00 |
| N30 | Luxury steering wheel (S87; NC w/T87, U87; NA w/W87) | NC |
| N33 | Tilt steering | 72.00 |
| N65 | Stowaway spare tire | NC |

| UPC | Description | Retail Price |
|-----|-------------|-------------:|
| N67 | Body-color Rally II wheels w/4 trim rings | |
| | S87 wo/N65 | 136.00 |
| | S87 w/N65 | 117.00 |
| | T87 w/N65 | 79.00 |
| | T87 wo/N65 | 98.00 |
| | U87, W87 | NC |
| N95 | Wire wheel covers | |
| | S87 | 146.00 |
| | T87 | 108.00 |
| N98 | 4 argent silver Rally II wheels w/trim rings | |
| | S87 wo/N65 | 136.00 |
| | T87 w/N65 | 79.00 |
| | T87 wo/N65 | 98.00 |
| | U87, W87 | NC |
| P01 | Deluxe wheel covers (S87) | 38.00 |
| QBP | FR78–15 white-letter steel-belted radial tires (S87, T87) | |
| | W/N65 | 49.00 |
| | Wo/N65 | 61.00 |
| QBU | FR78–15 black-sidewall steel-belted radial tires (S87, T87) | NC |
| QBW | FR78–15 white-sidewall steel-belted radial tires (S87, T87) | |
| | W/N65 | 37.00 |
| | Wo/N65 | 46.00 |
| QBX | GR70–15 black-sidewall steel-belted radial tires | NC |
| QCY | GR70–15 white-sidewall steel-belted radial tires (U87, W87) | 51.00 |
| UA1 | HD battery | 20.00 |
| UM1 | AM radio w/8 track player | 233.00 |
| UM2 | AM/FM stereo radio w/8 track player | 341.00 |
| UN3 | AM/FM radio w/cassette | 351.00 |
| UN9 | Radio Accommodation Package (NC w/opt radios) | 27.00 |
| UP5 | AM/FM radio w/40 channel CB radio (required w/U80) | 436.00 |
| UP6 | AM/FM stereo radio w/40 channel CB radio | 518.00 |
| UY8 | AM/FM stereo w/digital clock (NA w/W87, w/U35) | 392.00 |
| U35 | Electric clock (NA w/Rally gauges) | 22.00 |
| U58 | AM/FM stereo radio | 236.00 |
| U63 | AM radio | 83.00 |
| U69 | AM/FM radio | 154.00 |
| U80 | Rear seat speaker (w/UP5, U63, U69 only) | 24.00 |
| VJ9 | Calif emissions systems | 75.00 |
| V02 | Supercooling radiator | |
| | W/C60 | 31.00 |
| | Wo/C60 | 56.00 |
| WS6 | Trans Am Special Performance Package | |
| | W/W72 | 324.00 |

|     | W/L80 | 249.00 |
| WW7 | Hood decal (W87 wo/Y82, Y84, Y88; | |
|     | NC w/Y82, Y84, Y88) | 66.00 |
| WW8 | Rally cluster w/clock & tachometer | |
|     | Exc W87 | 123.00 |
|     | W87 | NC |
| WY9 | Hurst hatch roof | |
|     | Wo/Y82 | 625.00 |
|     | W/Y82 | NC |
| W50 | Formula Appearance Package (U87 only) | 137.00 |
| W60 | Sky Bird Appearance Package (T87) | |
|     | W/velour Lombardy cloth | 461.00 |
|     | W/vinyl doeskin trim | 430.00 |
| W63 | Rally cluster & clock (exc W87) | 63.00 |
| W68 | Red Bird Appearance Package (T87) | |
|     | W/velour Lombardy cloth | 465.00 |
|     | W/vinyl doeskin trim | 430.00 |
| W72 | 6.6 L V-8 4V engine (NA w/NA6, VJ9; required | |
|     | w/automatic transmission or M21) | |
|     | U87 | 280.00 |
|     | W87 | 75.00 |
| YJ8 | 4 painted cast-aluminum wheels | |
|     | W/S87 | 290.00 |
|     | T87 wo/W60 | 252.00 |
| Y82 | Black Special Edition built at Norwood | |
|     | (W87 only) | 1,259.00 |
| Y84 | Black Special Edition built at Van Nuys | |
|     | (W87 only) | 1,259.00 |
| Y88 | Gold Special Edition (W87 only) | 1,263.00 |
| Y90 | Custom Trim Group | |
|     | W/doeskin vinyl (U87, W87) | 99.00 |
|     | W/Lombardy cloth (U87, W87) | 134.00 |
|     | W/Lombardy cloth (T87, wo/W60) | 35.00 |
|     | W/Lombardy cloth (T87, w/W60) | NC |
| Y92 | Lamp Group | 18.00 |

## Facts

Except for minor changes, the 1978 Firebird's appearance was the same as 1977's.

Both the standard interior and the custom interior were redesigned.

The Blue Bird option was available on the Esprit until it was replaced by a similar Red Bird option that was based on the color red.

The Formula came standard with Rally II wheels.

On the Trans Am, the W72 6.6 liter engine was tuned to produce an additional 20 hp. This engine, again, was not available on California Trans Ams. The Rally gauge cluster with tachometer and clock became a no-cost option. Standard was a tachometer-only cluster. Color choices expanded to eight for the Trans Am, and taillight bezels were painted on all Trans Ams at midyear.

The black-and-gold Special Edition came only with T-tops. A midyear introduction was the Gold Special Edition, painted in Solar Gold. Two types of T-tops had been used on the Special Editions since 1976. The Hurst panels, coded WY9 for 1978, were smaller and used bright trim around the window cutouts. In 1978, T-tops were also supplied by Fisher Body. These usually had dark trim and were coded CC1.

The Trans Am's rear sway bar diameter was decreased to 0.625 in.

Available on the Trans Am was the WS6 Trans Am Special Performance Package. It consisted of 15x8 in. snowflake wheels in either argent or gold, 225/70R15 raised white-letter radial tires, and the rear sway bar's diameter increased to 0.75 in. The option did not include four-wheel disc brakes.

The Van Nuys plant again produced Firebirds in 1978.

*1978 Firebird Red Bird*

# Chapter 13

# 1979 Firebird

## Production

| Model | Manual | Automatic | Total |
|---|---|---|---|
| 2 dr base 6 & 8 cyl | | | 38,642 |
| 2 dr Esprit 6 & 8 cyl | | | 30,853 |
| 2 dr Formula 8 cyl | | | 24,850 |
| 2 dr Trans Am w/301 ci 8 cyl | 1,590 | 7,015 | 8,605 |
| 2 dr Trans Am w/400 ci 8 cyl | 2,485 | — | 2,485 |
| 2 dr Trans Am w/403 ci 8 cyl | — | 48,488 | 48,488 |
| 2 dr Trans Am w/301 ci 8 cyl* | 1,530 | 3,301 | 4,831 |
| 2 dr Trans Am w/400 ci 8 cyl* | 2,917 | — | 2,917 |
| 2 dr Trans Am w/403 ci 8 cyl* | — | 30,728 | 30,728 |
| 2 dr Trans Am w/301 ci 8 cyl† | 213 | 360 | 573 |
| 2 dr Trans Am w/400 ci 8 cyl† | 1,107 | — | 1,107 |
| 2 dr Trans Am w/403 ci 8 cyl† | — | 9,874 | 9,874 |
| 2 dr Trans Am w/400 ci 8 cyl‡ | 1,817 | — | 1,817 |
| 2 dr Trans Am w/403 ci 8 cyl‡ | — | 5,683 | 5,683 |
| Total | | | 211,453 |

*Trans Am with/T-top.
†Trans Am Special Edition with/T-top.
‡Trans Am Tenth Anniversary Edition.

## Serial Numbers

**Description**
2W87Z9N100001
2—Pontiac
W—Firebird body series (S = base, T = Esprit, U = Formula,
  W = Trans Am, X = Tenth Anniversary Trans Am)
87—Body style (87 = 2 dr coupe)
Z—engine code
9—last digit of model year (9 = 1979)
N—assembly plant (N = Norwood, L = Van Nuys)
100001—consecutive sequence number

**Location**
On plate attached to left side of dash, visible through windshield.

## Engine VIN Codes
A—3.8 L Buick
W, Y—4.9 L
G—5.0 L Chevrolet
L—5.0 L Chevrolet
Z—6.6 L
K—6.6 L Oldsmobile

## Engine Identification Codes
NL, RX, RY—3.8 L V-6 2 bbl 105 hp manual or automatic
PWA, PWB—4.9 L V-8 2 bbl 135 hp manual
PX4, PX6, PXP, PXR—5.0 L V-8 2 bbl 150 hp automatic
DN2, DNF, DNJ, DNK—5.0 L V-8 2 bbl 135 hp manual or automatic
DRJ, DRY—5.7 L V-8 4 bbl 170 hp manual or automatic
PWH—6.6 L V-8 4 bbl 220 hp manual
Q6, QE, QJ, QK, QL, TF—6.6 L V-8 4 bbl 185 hp automatic

## Pontiac Carburetors
4.9 L 302 ci 135 hp—17059160
4.9 L 301 ci 150 hp manual—17059271
4.9 L 301 ci 150 hp automatic—17059272
6.6 L 400 ci—17059263

## Pontiac Head Castings
4.9 L 301 ci 135 hp—01
4.9 L 301 ci 150 hp—02
6.6 L 400 ci—6X

## Exterior Color Codes

| | | | |
|---|---|---|---|
| Cameo White | 11 | Sundance Yellow | 51 |
| Platinum | 15 | Sierra Copper | 63 |
| Dark Charcoal | 16 | Heritage Brown | 69 |
| Starlight Black | 19 | Mayan Red | 75 |
| Atlantis Blue | 24 | Carmine | 77 |
| Nocturne Blue | 29 | Redbird Red | 80 |
| Solar Gold | 50 | | |

## Standard Interior Trim Codes

| Color | Vinyl Buckets | Custom Vinyl Buckets | Custom Cloth Buckets |
|---|---|---|---|
| Oyster | 12R1 | 12N1 | — |
| Black | 19R1 | 19N1 | 19B1 |
| Blue | — | 24N1 | 24B1 |
| Camel Tan | 62R1 | 62N1 | 62B1 |
| Carmine | 74R1 | 74N1 | 74B1 |
| Oyster/Blue trim | 12R1/24X | 12N1/24X | — |
| Oyster/Gray trim | 12R1/16X | 12N1/16X | — |
| Oyster/Black trim | 12R1/19X | 12N1/19X | — |
| Oyster/Camel trim | 12R1/62X | 12N1/62X | — |
| Oyster/Carmine trim | — | 12N1/74X | — |

## Vinyl Top Color Codes

| | | | |
|---|---|---|---|
| White | 11 | Green | 44 |
| Silver | 13 | Camel | 63 |
| Black | 19 | Claret | 76 |
| Blue | 21 | Gray | 85 |

# Options

| UPC | Description | Retail Price |
|-----|-------------|-------------:|
| | 2 dr coupe | $5,260.00 |
| | 2 dr coupe Esprit | 5,638.00 |
| | 2 dr coupe Formula | 6,564.00 |
| | 2 dr coupe Trans Am | 6,883.00 |
| | 2 dr coupe Trans Am Limited Edition | 10,620.00 |
| AK1 | Custom seatbelts | NC |
| AU3 | Power door locks | 86.00 |
| A01 | Tinted glass | 64.00 |
| A31 | Power window (required w/D55) | 132.00 |
| A90 | Remote control rear deck lid release | 24.00 |
| BS1 | Added acoustical insulation (S87, U87, W87; std w/T87) | 31.00 |
| B18 | Custom Trim Group | |
| | S87, W87, w/vinyl doeskin trim | 108.00 |
| | U87, W87 w/hobnail velour cloth trim | 150.00 |
| | T87, w/W68, hobnail velour cloth trim | 42.00 |
| B37 | Color-keyed front & rear floor mats | 25.00 |
| B80 | Roof drip moldings (wo/canopy top; all exc T87) | 24.00 |
| B83 | Rocker panel moldings (NA w/U87, W87; std w/T87) | 18.00 |
| B84 | Vinyl bodyside moldings | 43.00 |
| B85 | Windowsill & rear hood moldings (all exc T87 & W87 w/Y84) | 26.00 |
| B93 | Door edge guards | 13.00 |
| B96 | Wheel opening moldings (S87 only) | 22.00 |
| CB7 | Canopy top (NA on W87, X87, T87 w/W68) | 116.00 |
| CC1 | Hatch roof w/removable panels (W87 wo/Y84) | 655.00 |
| CD4 | Controlled-cycle windshield wipers | 38.00 |
| C49 | Electric rear window defroster | 99.00 |
| C60 | Custom AC | 529.00 |
| C95 | Dome reading lamp | 19.00 |
| D34 | RH visor vanity mirror | 6.00 |
| D35 | Dual sport OSRV mirrors, LH remote control (S87 only) | 43.00 |
| D53 | Hood bird decal (W87 wo/Y84) | 95.00 |
| D55 | Console (required w/automatic transmission; std in U87, W87; S87, T87) | 80.00 |
| D80 | Rear deck spoiler (S87, T87, U87 wo/W50) | 57.00 |
| D98 | Vinyl accent stripes (S87, T87) | 54.00 |
| G80 | Limited-slip differential (std w/W87, X87; on S87, T87, U87) | 63.00 |
| JL2 | Power brakes (required w/V-8, V-6, C60; std w/U87, W87) | 76.00 |
| J65 | 4 wheel power disc brakes (U87, W87 wo/Special Edition Package) | 150.00 |
| K05 | Engine block heater | 15.00 |
| K30 | Cruise control (required w/MX1; NA w/L78) | 103.00 |
| K81 | HD 63 amp alternator | |
| | Wo/C60, C49 | 32.00 |

| UPC | Description | Retail Price |
|-----|-------------|-------------|
| | W/C60, C49 | NC |
| LD5 | 3.8 L V-6 engine (S87, T87; NA w/NA6) | NC |
| LG3 | 5.0 L V-8 2V engine (required w/VJ9, automatic transmission) | |
| | S87, T87 | 270.00 |
| | U87 | NC |
| LM1 | 5.7 L V-8 4V engine (required w/NA6, automatic transmission) | |
| | S87, T87 | 425.00 |
| | U87 | 155.00 |
| L27 | 4.9 L V-8 2V engine (federal only; required with automatic transmission) | |
| | S87, T87 | 270.00 |
| | U87 | NC |
| L37 | 4.9 L V-8 4V engine (federal only) | |
| | S87, T87 | 355.00 |
| | U87 | 85.00 |
| | W87 | (195.00) |
| L78 | Trans Am 6.6 L V-8 4V engine (federal only; required w/M21, WS6) | |
| | U87 | 370.00 |
| | W87, X87 | 90.00 |
| MM3 | 3 speed manual transmission (required w/V-6; NA w/VJ9) | NC |
| MX1 | Turbo Hydra-matic automatic transmission (required w/D55; NA w/L78) | |
| | S87, T87 | 355.00 |
| | U87, W87, X87 | NC |
| M21 | Close-ratio 4 speed manual transmission (required w/L78, L37) | |
| | S87, T87 | 325.00 |
| | U87, W87, X87 | NC |
| NA6 | High-altitude emissions equipment | 35.00 |
| NK3 | Formula steering wheel | |
| | S87 | 68.00 |
| | T87 wo/W68 | 48.00 |
| N30 | Luxury steering wheel (S87) | 20.00 |
| N65 | Stowaway spare tire | NC |
| N67 | Body-color Rally II rims | |
| | S87 w/N65 | 126.00 |
| | S87 wo/N65 | 146.00 |
| | T87 w/N65 | 84.00 |
| | T87 wo/N65 | 104.00 |
| N90 | Cast-aluminum wheels | |
| | S87 | 310.00 |
| | T87 wo/W68 | 268.00 |
| | T87 w/W68 | 184.00 |
| N95 | Wire wheel covers | |
| | S87 | 157.00 |
| | T87 | 115.00 |

| | | |
|---|---|---:|
| N98 | Argent silver Rally II rims | |
| | S87 w/N65 | 126.00 |
| | S87 wo/N65 | 146.00 |
| | T87 w/N65 | 84.00 |
| | T87 wo/N65 | 104.00 |
| P01 | Deluxe wheel cover (S87) | 42.00 |
| QBP | FR78–15 white-letter steel-belted radial tires (S87, T87) | |
| | Wo/N65 | 64.00 |
| | W/N65 | 52.00 |
| QBU | FR78–15 blackwall steel-belted radial tires (S87, T87) | NC |
| QBW | FR78–15 white-letter steel-belted radial tires (S87, T87) | |
| | Wo/N65 | 48.00 |
| | W/N65 | 39.00 |
| QGQ | 225/70R–15 blackwall steel-belted radial tires (U87, W87, X87) | NC |
| QGR | 225/70R–15 white-letter steel-belted radial tires (U87, W87 w/WS6) | 53.00 |
| UA1 | HD battery | 21.00 |
| UM1 | AM radio w/integral 8 track stereo player | 248.00 |
| UM2 | AM/FM stereo radio w/integral 8 track player | 345.00 |
| UN3 | AM/FM radio w/stereo cassette | 351.00 |
| UN9 | Radio Accommodation Package (wo/opt radio) | |
| | Wo/U83 | 29.00 |
| | W/U83 | 10.00 |
| UP5 | AM/FM radio w/CB radio (incl U83) | 492.00 |
| UP6 | AM/FM stereo radio w/integral 40 channel CB radio (incl U83) | 574.00 |
| UP8 | Dual rear speakers (w/UP5, U63, U69; std w/all others) | 38.00 |
| UY8 | AM/FM stereo radio w/digital clock | 402.00 |
| U17 | Rally gauges w/clock & tachometer | |
| | S87, T87 | 130.00 |
| | Std w/W87, X87; U87 | 63.00 |
| U35 | Electric clock (std w/W63; wo/W63) | 24.00 |
| U58 | AM/FM stereo radio | 236.00 |
| U63 | AM radio | 86.00 |
| U69 | AM/FM radio | 163.00 |
| U75 | Power antenna | |
| | Wo/opt radio | 87.00 |
| | Std w/UP5, UP6; w/others | 68.00 |
| U80 | Rear seat speaker (only w/UP5, U63, U69) | 25.00 |
| U83 | AM/FM tri-band power antenna | |
| | Wo/opt radio | 87.00 |
| | Std w/UP5, UP6; w/others | 68.00 |
| VJ9 | Calif emissions equipment | 83.00 |
| V02 | Supercooling radiator | |
| | W/C60; NA w/L80 w/WS6 or NA6 | 59.00 |
| | W/C60 | 32.00 |

| UPC | Description | Retail Price |
|-----|-------------|-------------:|
| WS6 | Special Performance Package | |
| | U87, W87 only; required w/L37, L78, L80 | 434.00 |
| | W87 w/Y84 | 250.00 |
| W50 | Formula Appearance Package (U87 only) | 92.00 |
| W63 | Rally gauge cluster w/clock (V-8 only; | |
| | std w/U87; S87, T87) | 67.00 |
| W68 | Red Bird Appearance Package (T87) | |
| | W/hobnail cloth trim | 491.00 |
| | W/doeskin vinyl trim | 449.00 |
| Y84 | Special Edition Appearance Package (W87) | |
| | Wo/CC1 | 674.00 |
| | W/CC1 | 1,329.00 |

## Facts

The Firebird received another facelift in 1979, one that was to last until the second-generation Firebirds were finally replaced in 1982. The taillight panel got a new full-width look. Formulas and Trans Ams got opaque covers for a blacked-out look. Other changes included new wheel covers and interior trim.

The Formula's standard features were changed. The Trans Am rear spoiler went back to the option list, but the Formula steering wheel replaced the luxury cushion one used in 1978. The Rally gauge cluster was standard, and an engine-turned dash panel replaced the former wood-grain type. Standard tires were 225/70R-15 steel-belted blackwalls on Rally II rims.

The W50 Formula Appearance Package with its two-color paint and large Formula lettering continued, but the rear deck lid spoiler was included.

Four-wheel power disc brakes were optional on the Formula or Trans Am and were part of the WS6 Special Performance Package as well.

The Oldsmobile 6.6 liter (403 ci) engine was standard equipment on the Trans Am teamed with the automatic transmission. Optional was the Pontiac-built 4.9 liter (301 ci) V-8 as a credit option. The W72 was optionally available as well, with the manual M21 four-speed transmission only.

The Pontiac-built W72 400 ci V-8s were actually leftover engines built during the 1978 model year and stockpiled for 1979 use.

The Trans Am Special Edition was available in black only. T-tops were of the CC1 Fisher Body variety. The T-tops were a delete option.

Commemorating the tenth anniversary of the Trans Am was the Tenth Anniversary Edition. The silver paint was complemented with charcoal gray around the windows, windshield, T-top and rear window and highlighted with red, white and charcoal pinstripes. Charcoal gray was also used on the bumpers and shaker scoop. The Tenth Anniversary got distinctive 15x8 in. finned turbo wheels made by Appliance, special decals and a silver leather interior. The hood bird decal was larger than the usual optional decal.

The Tenth Anniversary was loaded to the gills with options that included most regular Trans Am options. Power windows, locks, antenna, trunk release, tilt steering wheel, quartz-halogen headlights, air conditioning, AM/FM eight track and four-wheel disc brakes were just some of the standard features.

The only engines available were the Oldsmobile 6.6 liter or the Pontiac-built 6.6 liter on the Tenth Anniversary.

Several Tenth Anniversary cars were used as pace cars in the 1979 Daytona 500.

Other Firebird improvements included a column-mounted headlight dimmer switch and convex glass on the right-hand outside rearview mirror.

*1979 Firebird Formula*

# Chapter 14

# 1980 Firebird

## Production

| | |
|---|---:|
| 2 dr base 6 & 8 cyl | 29,811 |
| 2 dr Esprit 6 & 8 cyl | 17,277 |
| 2 dr Formula 8 cyl | 9,356 |
| 2 dr Trans Am w/4.9 L 8 cyl | 25,714 |
| 2 dr Trans Am w/4.9 L Turbo 8 cyl | 16,476 |
| 2 dr Trans Am w/5.0 L 8 cyl | 3,006 |
| 2 dr Trans Am Turbo Indy Pace Car 8 cyl | 5,700 |
| Total | 107,340 |

## Serial Numbers

**Description**
2W87TAN100001
2—Pontiac
W—Firebird body series (S = base, T = Esprit, U = Formula,
   W = Trans Am, X = Indy Pace Car)
87—body style (87 = 2 dr coupe)
T—engine code
A—model year (A = 1980)
N—assembly plant (N = Norwood, L = Van Nuys)
10001—consecutive sequence number

**Location**
   On plate attached to left side of dash, visible through windshield.

## Engine VIN Codes

| | |
|---|---|
| A—3.8 L | T—4.9 L Turbo |
| W—4.9 L | H—5.0 L |
| Y—4.9 L | |

## Engine Identification Codes

MS, MX, OJ, OK, OL, OM, ON, OZ—3.8 L V-6 2 bbl 115 hp automatic
XN, YN—4.9 L V-8 2bbl 140 hp automatic
YL—4.9 L V-8 4 bbl 210 hp automatic
CEL, CEM—5.0 L V-8 4 bbl 150 hp automatic

## Exterior Color Codes

| | | | |
|---|---|---|---|
| Cameo White | 11 | Starlight Black | 19 |
| Platinum Silver | 15 | Tahoe Blue | 24 |

| | | | |
|---|---|---|---|
| Nightwatch Blue | 29 | Francisco Red | 71 |
| Yellow Bird Accent | 37 | Montreaux Maroon | 76 |
| Tahitian Yellow | 51 | Carousel Red | 79 |
| Yellow Bird Yellow | 56 | Fiero Bronze | 80 |
| Solar Gold | 57 | Ontario Gray | 84 |
| Barclay Brown | 67 | | |

## Standard Interior Trim Codes

| Color | Vinyl Buckets | Custom Vinyl Buckets | Custom Cloth Buckets |
|---|---|---|---|
| Oyster | 12R1 | 12N1 | — |
| Black | 19R1 | 19N1 | 19B1 |
| Blue | 26R1 | 26N1 | 26B1 |
| Camel Tan | 62R1 | 62N1 | 62B1 |
| Carmine | 74R1 | 74N1 | 74B1 |
| Oyster/Blue trim | 12R1/24X | 12N1/26X | — |
| Oyster/Gray trim | 12R1/16X | 12N1/16X | — |
| Oyster/Black trim | 12R1/19X | 12N1/19X | — |
| Oyster/Camel trim | 12R1/62X | 12N1/62X | — |
| Oyster/Carmine trim | — | 12N1/74X | — |

### Vinyl Top Color Codes

| | | | |
|---|---|---|---|
| White | 11 | Green | 44 |
| Silver | 13 | Camel | 63 |
| Black | 19 | Claret | 76 |
| Blue | 21 | Gray | 85 |

## Options

| UPC | Description | Retail Price |
|---|---|---|
| | 2 dr coupe | $5,948.00 |
| | 2 dr coupe Esprit | 6,311.00 |
| | 2 dr coupe Formula | 7,256.00 |
| | 2 dr coupe Trans Am | 7,480.00 |
| AK1 | Custom seatbelts (exc T87 wo/B18) | 25.00 |
| AU3 | Power door locks | 93.00 |
| AO1 | Tinted glass | 68.00 |
| A31 | Power windows | 143.00 |
| A90 | Remote control deck lid release | 26.00 |
| BS1 | Added acoustical insulation (std w/T87) | 34.00 |
| B18 | Custom Trim Group | |
| | V87, W87 w/vinyl doeskin trim | 142.00 |
| | V87, W87 w/hobnail cloth trim | 187.00 |
| | T87 w/hobnail cloth trim wo/W73 | 45.00 |
| B37 | Color-keyed front & rear floor mats | 27.00 |
| B80 | Scalp moldings (std w/T87, W87 w/Y84) | 26.00 |
| B83 | Rocker panel molding (S87 only; std w/T87; NA w/others) | 20.00 |
| B84 | Color-keyed bodyside moldings | 46.00 |
| B85 | Windowsill & rear hood moldings (std w/T87, W87 w/Y84) | 28.00 |

| UPC | Description | Retail Price |
|---|---|---|
| B93 | Door edge guards | 14.00 |
| B96 | Wheel opening moldings (std w/T87; NA w/others) | 24.00 |
| CC1 | Hatch roof (wo/Y84; std w/Y84) | 695.00 |
| CD4 | Controlled-cycle windshield wipers | 41.00 |
| C49 | Electric rear window defroster | 107.00 |
| C60 | AC | 566.00 |
| C95 | Dome reading lamp | 21.00 |
| D34 | Visor vanity mirror | 7.00 |
| D35 | Sport OSRV mirrors, LH remote control (S87) | 47.00 |
| D53 | Hood decal (wo/Y84; std w/Y84) | 120.00 |
| D80 | Rear deck spoiler | |
| | S87, T87 | 62.00 |
| | V87, wo/W73 | 62.00 |
| | V87 w/W73, V87, W87 | NC |
| D98 | Vinyl tape stripes (S87 & T87 wo/W50 or W73 only) | 58.00 |
| G80 | Limited-slip differential (all exc W87) | 68.00 |
| JL2 | Power front disc & rear drum brakes (S87; T87; std w/others) | 81.00 |
| J65 | 4 wheel power disc brakes (V87, W87 w/G80) | |
| | Wo/WS6 | 162.00 |
| | W/WS6 | NC |
| K05 | Engine block heater | 16.00 |
| K30 | Cruise control (required w/MX1; w/V-6 required w/JL2) | 112.00 |
| K81 | HD 63 amp alternator | |
| | Wo/C49, C60 | 36.00 |
| | W/C49, C60 | NC |
| LD5 | 3.8 L V-6 engine (S87, T87; NA w/VJ9) | NC |
| LG4 | 5.0 L V-8 engine | |
| | Required w/VJ9 & C60; S87, T87 | 195.00 |
| | Required w/VJ9 & C60; adds dual resonators; V87 | NC |
| | Deletes std chrome splitters; W87 | (180.00) |
| LU8 | 4.9 L Turbo engine (NA w/VJ9) | |
| | W87 | 350.00 |
| | V87 incl dual resonators | 530.00 |
| L37 | 4.9 L V-8 engine (NA w/VJ9) | |
| | S87, T87; incl chrome splitter | 180.00 |
| | V87 | NC |
| | W87; less dual resonators | (180.00) |
| MX1 | Automatic transmission (S87, T87) | 358.00 |
| NK3 | Formula steering wheel | |
| | S87 | 74.00 |
| | T87 wo/W73 | 52.00 |
| | T87 w/W73, V87, W87 | NC |
| N18 | Wheel Cover Locking Package (w/N95 only) | 35.00 |
| N30 | Luxury cushion steering wheel (S87) | 22.00 |
| N33 | Tilt steering wheel | 81.00 |
| N65 | Stowaway spare tire | NC |

| | | |
|---|---|---:|
| N67 | Body-color Rally II wheels & 4 trim rings | |
| | S87 w/N65 | 136.00 |
| | S87 wo/N65 | 158.00 |
| | T87 w/N65 | 91.00 |
| | T87 wo/N65 | 113.00 |
| | V87, W87 | NC |
| N90 | 4 cast-aluminum wheels | |
| | S87 | 336.00 |
| | T87 wo/W73 | 291.00 |
| N95 | Wire wheel covers | |
| | S87 | 171.00 |
| | T87 | 126.00 |
| N98 | Rally II wheels & 4 trim rings | |
| | S87 w/N65 | 136.00 |
| | S87 wo/N65 | 158.00 |
| | T87 w/N65 | 91.00 |
| | T87 wo/N65 | 113.00 |
| | V87, W87 | NC |
| P01 | Deluxe wheel covers (S87) | 45.00 |
| QGR | 205/75R15 white-letter steel belted radial tires | |
| | w/RTS (V87, W87 wo/WS6) | 68.00 |
| QJU | 205/75R15 black steel-belted radial tires | |
| | S87, T87) | NC |
| QJW | 205/75R15 whitewall steel-belted radial tires | |
| | (S87, T87) | |
| | Wo/N65 | 62.00 |
| | W/N65 | 50.00 |
| QMC | 205/75R15 white-letter steel-belted radial tires | |
| | (S87, T87) | |
| | Wo/N65 | 80.00 |
| | W/N65 | 64.00 |
| TR9 | Lamp Group | 22.00 |
| TT5 | Halogen headlights (high beam only) | 27.00 |
| UA1 | HD battery | 23.00 |
| UM1 | AM radio w/integral 8 track stereo tape player | 249.00 |
| UM2 | AM/FM stereo radio w/integral 8 track | |
| | stereo tape player | 272.00 |
| UM7 | AM/FM ETR radio w/Seek-&-Scan | |
| | (incl digital clock) | 375.00 |
| UN9 | Radio Accommodation Package | |
| | (std w/opt radio) | |
| | Wo/U75, U83 | 29.00 |
| | W/U75, U83 | 10.00 |
| UP6 | AM/FM stereo w/40 channel CB radio | |
| | (incl U83) | 525.00 |
| UP8 | Dual front & rear speakers (w/U63, U69 only) | 43.00 |
| UQ1 | Dual extended-range rear speakers | |
| | W/U63, U69 | 68.00 |
| | W/UM1, U58, UN3, UM2, UP6 | 25.00 |
| | W/UM7 | NC |
| UR4 | Turboboost gauge (required w/LU8) | 40.00 |

| UPC | Description | Retail Price |
|-----|-------------|-------------|
| UX6 | Dual front speakers (w/U63, U69 only) | 14.00 |
| U17 | Rally gauges | |
| | S87, T87; required w/V-8 | 159.00 |
| | V87; std w/W87 | 68.00 |
| U35 | Electric quartz clock (wo/Rally gauges) | 30.00 |
| U58 | AM/FM stereo radio | 192.00 |
| U63 | AM radio | 97.00 |
| U69 | AM/FM radio | 153.00 |
| U75 | Power antenna (NA w/UP6) | |
| | Wo/opt radios | 70.00 |
| | W/opt radios | 51.00 |
| U80 | Rear seat speaker (w/U63, U69 only) | 20.00 |
| U83 | AM/FM/CB tri-band power antenna | |
| | Wo/opt radio | 93.00 |
| | W/opt radio | 74.00 |
| VJ9 | Calif emissions | 250.00 |
| V02 | Supercooling radiator (NA w/LU8) | |
| | W/C60 | 35.00 |
| | Wo/C60 | 64.00 |
| WS6 | Special Appearance Package (V87 w/L37, LG4, LU8, W72) | 481.00 |
| W50 | Formula Appearance Package (V87 only) | 100.00 |
| W63 | Rally gauges (S87, T87; required w/V-8; std w/V87) | 91.00 |
| W72 | 4.9 L E/C engine (NA w/VJ9) | |
| | V87 incl dual resonators | 180.00 |
| | W87 | NC |
| W73 | Yellow Bird (V87 only) | |
| | W/velour hobnail trim | 550.00 |
| | W/vinyl doeskin trim | 505.00 |
| Y84 | Special Edition (W87 only) | |
| | Wo/CC1 | 748.00 |
| | W/CC1 | 1,443.00 |

## Facts

The 1980 styling was a carryover from 1979 styling, but option and equipment changes were made on all Firebird models.

The base Firebird's standard equipment included the center console. The standard engine was the Buick 3.8 liter V-6, except for California cars, which got the Chevrolet 5.0 liter V-8. The optional engine was the 5.0 liter Chevrolet V-8 in all states except California.

The Esprit got the same engine options as the base model. A Yellow Bird option replaced the Red Bird. A camel tan Formula steering wheel with gold spokes was standard with the Yellow Bird until November 20, 1979, when it was replaced with one that had black-painted spokes. The same applied for the Special Edition Trans Am.

The Formula got chrome side-splitter exhaust extensions and the black taillight lenses. The standard engine was the Pontiac-built 4.9 liter V-8 except in California, which got the 5.0 liter Chevrolet V-8. Other optional engines were the 4.9 liter 155 hp E/C and the turbocharged version of the 4.9 liter, rated at 210 hp. The turbo-charged 4.9 liter engine came with a special hood with an off-center hood bulge necessitated by the turbocharger. A Turbo 4.9 decal was located on the left side of the hood bulge. Formulas without the 4.9 liter Turbo got the usual twin-scoop hood.

Engine availability on the Trans Am was the same as on the Formula, except that the 4.9 liter E/C engine was standard on forty-nine-state cars. Trans Ams equipped with the 4.9 liter Turbo engine got the special off-center hood and a different big bird decal. The bird in this decal had a longer wingspan and its head was turned to the left. The 4.9 liter Turbo engine was not available for California-bound Firebirds.

The black-and-gold Special Edition was still available, but it was the Turbo Indy Pace Car that got all the attention. Painted white with gray highlights, the car came with oyster-and-black vinyl-and-cloth bucket seats, a silver-tinted T-top, air conditioning, power windows, the WS6 Special Appearance Package, four-wheel disc brakes and the 15x8 in. finned turbo wheels painted white.

Standard Trans Am wheels were the Rally IIs with trim rings. Body-color Rally IIs and the snowflake cast-aluminum wheels were optional. The turbo cast-aluminum wheels were optional on the Formula and Trans Am only in conjunction with the WS6 Special Appearance Package and 4.9 liter Turbo engine. California cars could get the wheels with the WS6 package, as the 4.9 liter Turbo was not certified for sale in California.

The Trans Am Turbo was also used as the Daytona 500 pace car.

All 1980 Firebirds came with automatic transmissions.

*1980 Firebird Turbo Trans Am Pace Car*

# Chapter 15

# 1981 Firebird

## Production

| Model | Manual | Automatic | Total |
|---|---|---|---|
| 2 dr base 6 & 8 cyl | | | 20,541 |
| 2 dr Esprit 6 & 8 cyl | | | 10,938 |
| 2 dr Formula 8 cyl | | | 5,927 |
| 2 dr Trans Am w/4.9 L E/C 8 cyl | — | 10,877 | 10,877 |
| 2 dr Trans Am w/4.9 L Turbo 8 cyl | — | 13,578 | 13,578 |
| 2 dr Trans Am w/5.0 L 8 cyl | 7,038 | — | 7,038 |
| 2 dr Trans Am NASCAR Turbo Pace Car 8 cyl | — | 2,000 | 2,000 |
| Total | | | 70,899 |

## Serial Numbers

**Description**
1G2AS37A1BN100001
1—United States
G—General Motors
2—Pontiac
A—restraint type (A = manual belts)
S—Firebird body series (S = base, T =Esprit, V = Formula,
 W = Trans Am)
37—body style (37 = 2 dr coupe)
A—engine code
1—check digit, which varies
B—model year (B = 1981)
N—assembly plant (N = Norwood, L = Van Nuys)
100001—consecutive sequence number

**Location**
 On plate attached to left side of dash, visible through windshield.

## Engine VIN Codes
A—3.8 L
S—4.3 L

W—4.9 L E/C
T—4.9 L Turbo
G, H, S—5.0 L

## Engine Identification Codes
LZ, NA, NB, NC, ND, NF, NJ, NL, NZ, RA, RB, RC, RD, RK, RL—3.8
 L V-6 2 bbl manual/automatic
AU, AW, AZ, BA, DB DC, DH, DJ—4.3 L V-8 2 bbl manual or
 automatic

BD, BJ—4.9 L V–8 2 bbl automatic
4.9 L V–8 4 bbl 210 hp automatic
5.0 L V–8 4 bbl 150 hp automatic

# Exterior Color Codes

| | | | |
|---|---|---|---|
| White | 11 | Gold Metallic | 54 |
| Silver Metallic | 16 | Yellow | 56 |
| Black | 19 | Orange Metallic | 57 |
| Bright Blue Metallic | 20 | Dark Brown Metallic | 67 |
| Light Blue Metallic | 21 | Bright Red | 75 |
| Dark Blue Metallic | 29 | Dark Maroon Metallic | 77 |
| Bright Yellow | 51 | Dark Charcoal Metallic | 84 |

# Standard Interior Trim Codes

| Color | Vinyl Buckets | Custom Vinyl Buckets | Custom Cloth Buckets |
|---|---|---|---|
| Silver | 15R1 | 15N1 | — |
| Black | 19R1 | 19N1 | 19B1 |
| Blue | 26R1 | 26N1 | 26B1/26D1 |
| Camel Tan | 64R1 | 64N1 | 64B1/64D1 |
| Red | 75R1 | 75N1 | 75B1 |

# Vinyl Top Color Codes

| | |
|---|---|
| White | 11 |
| Silver | 13 |
| Black | 19 |
| Blue | 29 |
| Waxberry | 36 |
| Jadestone | 45 |
| Sandstone | 63 |
| Doeskin | 64 |
| Maple | 77 |
| Slate | 85 |

# Options

| UPC | Description | Retail Price |
|---|---|---|
| | 2 dr coupe 6 cyl | $6,901.00 |
| | 2 dr coupe V-8 | 6,951.00 |
| | 2 dr coupe 6 cyl Esprit | 7,645.00 |
| | 2 dr coupe V-8 Esprit | 7,695.00 |
| | 2 dr coupe 6 cyl Formula | 7,854.00 |
| | 2 dr coupe V-8 Formula | 7,904.00 |
| | 2 dr coupe Trans Am | 8,322.00 |
| | 2 dr coupe Trans Am Turbo Special Edition | 12,257.00 |
| AK1 | Custom seatbelts | 26.00 |
| AU3 | Power door locks | 99.00 |
| A01 | Soft-Ray glass, all windows | 82.00 |
| A31 | Power windows | 152.00 |
| A51 | Bucket seats | 28.00 |

| UPC | Description | Retail Price |
|-----|-------------|-------------|
| A90 | Remote control deck lid release | 29.00 |
| BS1 | Added acoustical insulation | 36.00 |
| B18 | Custom trim option | 48.00–196.00 |
| B37 | Front & rear floor mats | 25.00 |
| B80 | Roof drip moldings | 27.00 |
| B83 | Rocker panel moldings | 23.00 |
| B84 | Bodyside moldings | 44.00 |
| B85 | Windowsill & rear hood edge moldings | 30.00 |
| B93 | Door edge guard moldings | 14.00 |
| B96 | Wheel opening moldings | 26.00 |
| CC1 | Hatch roof | 737.00 |
| CD4 | Controlled-cycle windshield wipers | 44.00 |
| C49 | Electric rear window defroster | 115.00 |
| C60 | Custom AC | 600.00 |
| C95 | Dome reading lamp | 21.00 |
| D34 | Visor vanity mirror | 7.00 |
| D35 | Sport OSRV mirror | 51.00 |
| D53 | Hood decal | 125.00 |
| D80 | Rear deck lid spoiler | 64.00 |
| D98 | Vinyl tape stripes | 61.00 |
| G80 | Limited-slip axle | 71.00–71.13 |
| J65 | Front & rear power disc brakes | 167.00 |
| K05 | Engine block heater | 17.00 |
| K35 | Cruise control | 145.00 |
| K73 | HD 70 amp alternator | 51.00 |
| LD5 | 3.8 L V-6 2V engine | NC |
| LG4 | 5.0 L V-8 4V engine | 75.00–(140.00) |
| LS5 | 4.3 L V-8 2V engine | 50.00 |
| LU8 | 4.9 L Turbo V-8 4V engine | 437.00–652.00 |
| L37 | 4.9 L E/C V-8 4V engine | 215.00 |
| MM3 | 3 speed manual transmission | NC |
| MM4 | 4 speed manual transmission | NC |
| MX1 | Automatic transmission | 370.00 |
| NK3 | Formula steering wheel | 55.00–78.00 |
| N18 | Wire wheel cover locks | 36.00 |
| N30 | Luxury cushion steering wheel | 23.00 |
| N33 | Tilt steering wheel | 88.00 |
| N90 | Turbo cast-aluminum wheels | 208.00–351.00 |
| N95 | Wire wheel covers | 130.00–179.00 |
| N96 | Body-color Rally II wheels & 4 trim rings | 94.00–143.00 |
| N98 | Silver Rally II wheels & 4 trim rings | 94.00–143.00 |
| P01 | Deluxe wheel covers | 179.00 |
| QJW | 205/75R15 whitewall steel-belted radial tires | 56.00 |
| QMC | 205/75R15 white-letter steel-belted radial tires | 74.00 |
| QQR | 225/70R15 white-letter steel-belted radial tires | 78.00 |
| TR9 | Lamp Group | 35.00 |
| TT5 | Halogen headlights | 29.00 |
| UA1 | HD battery | 22.00 |
| UM1 | AM radio w/integral 8 track stereo tape player | 231.00 |

| UM2 | AM/FM stereo radio w/integral 8 track stereo player | 252.00 |
|------|------|------|
| UM6 | AM/FM ETR stereo radio w/tape, clock, digital | 555.00 |
| UM7 | AM/FM ETR stereo radio w/Seek-&-Scan (incl digital) | 402.00 |
| UN3 | AM/FM ETR stereo radio w/tape (incl UQ1) | 289.00 |
| UN9 | Radio Accommodation Package | 29.00 |
| UP6 | AM/FM/CB stereo radio | 490.00 |
| UP8 | Dual front & rear speakers | 42.00 |
| UQ1 | Dual extended-range rear speakers | 25.00-67.00 |
| UQ3 | Audio power booster | 109.00 |
| UX6 | Dual front speakers | 15.00 |
| U17 | Rally gauges, clock, trip odometer & tachometer | 166.00 |
| U35 | Electric quartz clock | 30.00 |
| U58 | AM/FM stereo radio | 178.00 |
| U63 | AM radio | 90.00 |
| U69 | AM/FM radio | 142.00 |
| U75 | Power antenna | 70.00 |
| U80 | Dual rear speakers | 20.00 |
| U83 | Power antenna | 92.00 |
| VJ9 | Calif emissions | 46.00 |
| V02 | Supercooling radiator | 37.00-67.00 |
| WS6 | Special Performance Package | 372.00-580.00 |
| W50 | Formula Appearance Package | 212.00 |
| W63 | Rally gauges, clock & trip odometer | 95.00 |
| Y84 | Special Edition Appearance Package | 779.00-1,516.00 |

## Facts

The last of the second-generation Firebirds was essentially unchanged. The front grille was black with argent accents, and on the rear taillight panel, a white bird emblem was located on the fuel filler door.

All Firebird engines got GM's Computer Command Control system. With this, an onboard computer controlled all engine functions. Additionally, all Firebirds got automatic transmissions with computer-controlled-lockup torque converters.

The W50 Formula Appearance Package was modified slightly, but the large Formula lettering on the doors was still the trademark of the package. The rear deck lid spoiler was once again standard equipment with the Formula.

The 4.9 liter Turbo was again the high-performance Firebird engine. Available only on the Formula and Trans Am models, it still came with the offset hood. In the interior, Firebird Turbos got a turboboost gauge.

Required with the 4.9 liter Turbo were air conditioning, automatic transmission and four-wheel disc brakes.

On the Trans Am, the standard engine was the 4.9 liter E/C V-8. The Chevrolet 5.0 liter V-8 was available as a delete option and only with a four-speed manual. The 4.9 liter Turbo was optional. Trans Ams—and Formulas—so equipped did not get the chrome splitter exhaust outlets.

The black-and-gold Trans Am Special Edition was available with and without the T-top and with and without the 4.9 liter Turbo engine.

Similar to the 1980 Turbo Indy Pace Car was the NASCAR Turbo Pace Car. Painted Oyster White, it got black accents rather than the charcoal ones used on the 1980 Indy cars. In the interior, Recaro bucket seats finished in black and red were used.

For a short time, the last version of the Pontiac V-8 displacing 4.3 liter (265 ci) was standard on the Formula until production ceased in March 1981. Afterwards, the 3.8 liter Buick V-6 was standard.

*1981 Firebird Trans Am Turbo*

# Chapter 16

# 1982 Firebird

## Production

| | |
|---|---|
| 2 dr base | 41,683 |
| 2 dr S/E | 21,719 |
| 2 dr Trans Am | 52,960 |
| Total | 116,362 |

## Serial Numbers

**Description**
1G2AS87H1CN100001
1—United States
G—General Motors
2—Pontiac
A—restraint type (A = manual belts)
S—Firebird body series (S = base, W = Trans Am, X = S/E)
87—body style (87 = 2 dr coupe)
H—engine code
1—check digit, which varies
C—model year (C = 1982)
N—assembly plant (N = Norwood, L = Van Nuys)
100001—consecutive sequence number

**Location**
On plate attached to left side of dash, visible through windshield.

## Engine VIN Codes
F, 2, 5—2.5 L I-4
X, Z, 1—2.8 L V-6
H—5.0 L V-8 (LG4)
7—5.0 L V-8 (LU5)

## Engine Identification Codes
CFA, CFB, CFC, CFD, CFF, CFH, CFR, CFT, CFW, CFY, CFZ, CRA, CZR, CZS, CZT, CZU, CZW, CZX—5.0 L V-8 4 bbl 145 hp manual or automatic
CEJ, CFK, CFM, CFN—5.0 L V-8 TBI 165 hp automatic

## Exterior Color Codes

| | | | |
|---|---|---|---|
| White | 11 | Dark Jadestone Metallic | 49 |
| Silver Metallic | 16 | Gold Metallic | 55 |
| Black | 19 | Bright Red | 75 |
| Light Blue Metallic | 21 | Maroon Metallic | 78 |
| Dark Blue Metallic | 29 | Dark Charcoal Metallic | 84 |
| Light Jadestone Metallic | 45 | | |

## Interior Trim Codes

| | | | |
|---|---|---|---|
| Charcoal | 17 | Red Doeskin | 64 |
| Royal Blue | 22 | Dark Briar Brown | 67 |
| Light Sand Gray | 60 | | |

## Options

| UPC | Description | Retail Price |
|---|---|---|
| | 2 dr coupe 4 & 6 cyl | $7,996.00 & $8,121.00 |
| | 2 dr coupe S/E 6 & 8 cyl | 9,624.00 & 9,819.00 |
| | 2 dr coupe Trans Am | 9,658.00 |
| AC3 | 6 way power driver's seat | 197.00 |
| AK1 | Custom front & rear seatbelts & front shoulder straps | NC |
| AR9 | Bucket seats | 28.00 |
| AU3 | Power door locks | 106.00 |
| A01 | Soft-Ray glass, all windows | 88.00 |
| A31 | Power windows | 165.00 |
| A90 | Remote control deck lid release | 32.00 |
| BS1 | Added acoustical insulation | 39.00 |
| BX5 | Roof drip moldings | 29.00 |
| B20 | Luxury Trim Group | |
| | Base | 299.00-844.00 |
| | Trans Am | 299.00-844.00 |
| | S/E | 545.00 |
| B34 | Carpeted front floor mats | 20.00 |
| B35 | Carpeted rear floor mats | 15.00 |
| B48 | Luggage compartment trim | 123.00 |
| B57 | Custom Exterior Group | 73.00-134.00 |
| B80 | Roof drip moldings | 61.00 |
| B84 | Vinyl bodyside moldings | NA |
| B91 | Door edge guards | 15.00 |
| B93 | Bright door edge guards (base) | 15.00 |
| CC1 | Hatch roof w/removable glass panels | 790.00 |
| CD4 | Controlled-cycle windshield wiper system | 47.00 |
| C25 | Rear window wiper-washer system | 117.00 |
| C49 | Electric rear window defogger | 125.00 |
| C60 | Custom AC | 675.00 |
| C95 | Dome reading lamp | 22.00 |
| DG7 | Sport OSRV mirrors | 89.00-137.00 |
| D34 | RH visor vanity mirror | 7.00 |
| D35 | Sport OSRV mirrors | 48.00 |
| D42 | Cargo security screen | 64.00 |
| D80 | Rear deck spoiler | 69.00 |
| G80 | Limited-slip differential axle | 76.45-100.45 |
| J65 | Front & rear power disc brakes | 255.00 |
| K05 | Engine block heater | 18.00 |
| K35 | Cruise control w/resume feature | 155.00-165.00 |
| K73 | HD 70 amp generator | 51.00 |
| K81 | HD 63 amp generator | 51.00 |
| K99 | HD 85 amp generator | 51.00 |
| LC1 | 2.8 L 173 ci V-6 2 bbl engine | 125.08 |

| LG4 | 5.0 L 305 ci V-8 4 bbl engine | 170.00–195.00 |
|------|-------------------------------|---------------|
| LQ9 | 2.5 L 151 ci EFI L-4 engine | (125.00) |
| LU5 | Dual EFI Engine Package | 899.00 |
| MM4 | 4 speed manual transmission | NC |
| MX1 | Automatic transmission | 72.00–396.00 |
| N09 | Locking fuel filler door | 11.00 |
| N24 | 15x7 in. finned turbo cast-aluminum wheels | NC |
| N33 | Tilt steering wheel | 95.00 |
| N90 | Cast-aluminum wheels | 375.00 |
| N91 | Wire wheel covers w/Locking Package | 229.00 |
| PB4 | Wheel Locking Package | 16.00 |
| PE5 | Rally V wheel covers | 144.00 |
| P06 | Wheel trim rings | 37.00 |
| P20 | Bright aluminum wheel hubcap | NC |
| QVJ | 195/75R14 whitewall steel-belted radial tires | 126.60 |
| QXQ | 195/75R14 white-letter steel-belted radial tires | 148.60 |
| QXV | 195/75R14 blackwall steel-belted radial tires | 64.60 |
| QYA | 205/70R14 blackwall steel-belted radial tires | 123.76 |
| QYC | 205/70R14 white-letter steel-belted radial tires | 88.00–211.76 |
| QYF | 195/75R14 blackwall fiberglass-belted radial tires | NC |
| QYG | 195/75R14 whitewall fiberglass-belted radial tires | 62.00 |
| QYH | 215/65R15 white-letter steel-belted radial tires | 92.00 |
| QYZ | 215/65R15 blackwall steel-belted radial tires | NC |
| TR9 | Lamp Group | 45.00 |
| UA1 | HD battery | 25.00 |
| UE8 | Digital quartz clock | 60.00 |
| UM6 | Delco AM/FM ETR cassette system | 606.00 |
| UM7 | Delco AM/FM ETR stereo system | 438.00 |
| UN3 | Delco AM/FM stereo cassette system | 411.00 |
| UN9 | Radio Accommodation Package | 9.00–39.00 |
| UP8 | Dual front & rear speakers | 79.00 |
| U21 | Rally & instrument panel tachometer gauges | 149.00 |
| U58 | Delco AM/FM stereo radio system | 317.00 |
| U63 | Delco AM radio system | 102.00 |
| U69 | Delco AM/FM radio system | 232.00 |
| U75 | Power antenna | 55.00–85.00 |
| VJ9 | Calif emissions requirements | 65.00 |
| V08 | HD radiator | 40.00 |
| WS6 | Special Performance Package | 387.00–417.00 |
| WS7 | Special Performance Package (NA base) | 208.00–238.00 |
| Y84 | Recaro Trans Am option | 2,486.00–2,968.00 |
| Y99 | Rally tuned suspension | 408.00 |

**Facts**

Bringing the Firebird into the eighties was the totally redesigned and restyled third generation. Built on a shorter 101 in. wheelbase, it did not use a front subframe, as the previous two generations had, but was of a full unit-body construction. In the rear, coil springs replaced the leaf springs, and in the front, modified MacPherson struts were used.

Only one body style was available, a two-door hatchback coupe. The Firebird was available in three models: base, Special Edition (S/E) and Trans Am.

The base model came with a 2.5 liter four-cylinder engine and four-speed manual transmission. Standard features included power front disc brakes, power steering, console, Formula steering wheel and dual outside rearview mirrors.

The S/E got the Chevrolet 2.8 liter V-6 as standard equipment, black exterior accents, color-keyed moldings, aluminum wheels, an electric hatch and full-width hidden taillights.

The Trans Am came with a 5.0 liter V-8, black exterior accents, front fender extractors, wheel flares, a rear spoiler and aluminum wheels. Trans Am decals were located on the front fenders behind the wheelwells. Firebird bird decals were used on the sail panels and on the fuel filler door.

The Trans Am's standard V-8 got a four-barrel carburetor. The optional 165 hp version of the engine used dual throttle body (crossfire) injection, or TBI, for 165 hp output. Both engines used a single exhaust system with twin outlets. The 165 hp engine was available only with the automatic transmission.

Approximately 2,000 Trans Ams got the Recaro interior option. Available on black cars with gold accents, this included the Recaro seats, a T-top roof and the WS6 or WS7 performance package. The Recaro name was located on the door handles in gold lettering.

The WS6 package included four-wheel power disc brakes, Goodyear Eagle GT tires, 15x7 in. aluminum wheels, a limited-slip rear, special steering firmer springs and shocks, and larger-diameter sway bars—32 mm front and 21 mm rear.

*1982 Firebird S/E*

# Chapter 17

# 1983 Firebird

## Production

| | |
|---|---|
| 2 dr base | 32,020 |
| 2 dr S/E | 10,934 |
| 2 dr Trans Am | 31,930 |
| Total | 74,884 |

## Serial Numbers

**Description**
1G2AW87H1DN100001
1—United States
G—General Motors
2—Pontiac
A—restraint type (A = manual belts)
W—Firebird body series (S = base, W = Trans Am, X = S/E)
87—body style (87 = 2 dr coupe)
H—engine code
1—check digit, which varies
D—model year (D = 1983)
N—assembly plant (N = Norwood, L = Van Nuys)
100001—consecutive sequence number

**Location**
On plate attached to left side of dash, visible through windshield.

## Engine VIN Codes

| | |
|---|---|
| F—2.5 L I-4 | H—5.0 L V-8 (LG4) |
| I—2.8 L V-6 | S—5.0 L V-8 (LU5) |
| L—2.8 L V-6 | |

## Engine Identification Codes

D5B, D5C, D5D, D5F, D5H, D5N, D5R, DDB, DDC, DDD, DDF, DDH, DDJ, DDK, DDM, DDS, DDW—5.0 L V-8 4 bbl 145 hp manual or automatic
DDA, DDY, DUA, DUK, DWT—5.0 L V-8 TBI 165 hp automatic

## Exterior Color Codes

| | | | |
|---|---|---|---|
| White | 11 | Light Brown Metallic | 62 |
| Silver Sand Metallic | 15 | Dark Brown Metallic | 67 |
| Black | 19 | Bright Red | 75 |
| Light Royal Blue Metallic | 22 | Dark Sand Gray Metallic | 82 |
| Dark Royal Blue Metallic | 27 | | |

## Interior Trim Codes

| | | | |
|---|---|---|---|
| Charcoal | 17 | Red Doeskin | 64 |
| Royal Blue | 22 | Dark Briar Brown | 67 |
| Light Sand Gray | 60 | | |

## Options

| UPC | Description | Retail Price |
|---|---|---|
| | 2 dr coupe 4 & 6 cyl | $8,399.00 & $8,549.00 |
| | 2 dr coupe S/E 6 & 8 cyl | 10,322.00 & 10,397.00 |
| | 2 dr coupe Trans Am | 10,396.00 |
| AC3 | 6 way power seat | 210.00 |
| AK1 | Color-keyed seatbelts | 26.00 |
| AR9 | Bucket seats | 30.00 |
| AU3 | Power door locks | 120.00 |
| A01 | Soft-Ray glass, all windows | 105.00 |
| A31 | Power windows | 180.00 |
| A90 | Remote control deck lid release | 40.00 |
| BS1 | Added acoustical insulation | 40.00 |
| BX5 | Roof drip moldings | 29.00 |
| B20 | Luxury Trim Group | |
| | Luxury reclining bucket seats | 349.00 |
| | Lear-Siegler adjustable bucket seats | 400.00–749.00 |
| | Lear-Siegler adjustable bucket seats w/leather trim | 945.00–1,294.00 |
| B34 | Carpeted front floor mats | 20.00 |
| B35 | Carpeted rear floor mats | 15.00 |
| B48 | Luggage compartment trim | 123.00 |
| B57 | Custom Exterior Group | 112.00 |
| B80 | Roof drip moldings | 61.00 |
| B84 | Vinyl bodyside moldings | 55.00 |
| B91 | Door edge guards | 15.00 |
| B93 | Bright door edge guards (base) | 15.00 |
| CC1 | Hatch roof w/removable glass panels | 825.00 |
| CD4 | Controlled-cycle windshield wiper system | 49.00 |
| C25 | Rear window wiper-washer system | 120.00 |
| C49 | Electric rear window defogger | 135.00 |
| C60 | AC | 725.00 |
| C95 | Dome reading lamp | 23.00 |
| DE1 | Hinge-mounted louvered rear window sunshield | 210.00 |
| DG7 | LH & RH sport electric OSRV mirrors | 89.00–140.00 |
| DX1 | Hood appliqué | 38.00 |
| D34 | RH visor vanity mirror | 7.00 |
| D35 | Sport OSRV mirrors | 51.00 |
| D42 | Cargo security screen | 64.00 |
| D53 | Hood bird decal | NC |
| D80 | Rear deck spoiler | 70.00 |
| D98 | Vinyl sport stripes | 75.00 |
| G80 | Limited-slip differential axle | 95.43–100.43 |
| J65 | Front & rear power disc brakes | 274.00 |
| K05 | Engine block heater | 18.00 |

| | | |
|---|---|---|
| K35 | Cruise control w/resume feature | 170.00 |
| K64 | HD 78 amp generator | 25.00–51.00 |
| K81 | HD 66 amp generator | 51.00 |
| K99 | HD 85 amp generator | 25.00 |
| LC1 | 2.8 L V-6 2 bbl engine (base) | 150.00 |
| LG4 | 5.0 L V-8 4 bbl engine | |
| | Base | 350.00–375.00 |
| | S/E | 50.00–75.00 |
| | Trans Am | NC |
| LL1 | 2.8 L HO V-6 2 bbl engine | NC |
| LQ9 | 2.5 L EFI 4 cyl engine | |
| | Base | NC |
| | S/E | (300.00) |
| LU5 | 5.0 L Crossfire EFI V-8 Package | 858.00 |
| MM4 | 4 speed manual transmission | NC |
| MM5 | 5 speed manual transmission | 125.00 |
| MX0 | 4 speed automatic transmission | 295.00–525.00 |
| MX1 | 3 speed automatic transmission | 195.00–425.00 |
| NP5 | Leather-wrapped Formula steering wheel | 40.00 |
| N09 | Locking fuel filler door | 11.00 |
| N24 | Finned turbo cast-aluminum wheels | 325.00 |
| N33 | Tilt steering wheel | 105.00 |
| N90 | Cast-aluminum wheels | 225.00 |
| N91 | Wire wheel covers w/Locking Package | 185.00 |
| PB4 | Wheel Locking Package | 16.00–120.00 |
| PE5 | Rally V wheel covers | 95.00 |
| P06 | Wheel trim rings | 38.00 |
| QXQ | 195/75R14 white-letter steel-belted radial tires | 148.48 |
| QXV | 195/75R14 blackwall steel-belted radial tires | 64.48 |
| QYA | 205/70R14 blackwall steel-belted radial tires | 122.68 |
| QYC | 205/70R14 white-letter steel-belted radial tires | 88.00–210.68 |
| QYF | 195/75R14 blackwall fiberglass-belted radial tires | NC |
| QYG | 195/75R14 whitewall fiberglass-belted radial tires | 62.00 |
| QYH | 215/65R15 white-letter steel-belted radial tires | 93.40 |
| QYJ | 195/75R14 whitewall steel-belted radial tires | 126.48 |
| QYZ | 215/65R15 blackwall steel-belted radial tires | 1.40 |
| TR9 | Lamp Group | 34.00 |
| UA1 | HD battery | 25.00 |
| UL1 | AM/FM ETR stereo radio system w/clock | 287.00 |
| UL6 | AM radio system w/clock | 151.00 |
| UN9 | Radio Accommodation Package | 9.00–39.00 |
| UP8 | Dual rear speakers | 40.00 |

| UPC | Description | Retail Price |
|------|-------------|-------------:|
| UU6 | AM/FM ETR stereo radio w/cassette, Seek-&-Scan, graphic equalizer & clock | 590.00 |
| UU7 | AM/FM ETR stereo radio system w/cassette clock | 387.00 |
| UU9 | AM/FM ETR stereo radio system | 248.00 |
| U21 | Rally gauge cluster w/tachometer & trip odometer | 150.00 |
| U63 | AM radio system | 112.00 |
| U75 | Power antenna | 60.00-90.00 |
| VJ0 | Calif emissions requirements | 75.00 |
| V08 | HD cooling system | 40.00-70.00 |
| WS6 | Special Performance Package | 408.00 |
| Y84 | Special Edition Recaro Trans Am option | 3,610.00 |
| Y99 | Rally Tuned Suspension Handling Package | 50.00 |

## Facts

The 1983 Firebird's appearance was essentially unchanged from the 1982's.

The base Firebird got a new four-speed manual transmission with integral rail shifter. Also new were standard Rally wheels.

The S/E benefited from the new 2.8 liter HO V-6 engine with its 135 hp output. The new Borg-Warner T5 five-speed manual transmission was standard equipment. The 2.5 liter was a delete option and the 5.0 liter four-barrel was optional. The WS6 suspension package was available on the S/E. Also standard on the S/E was a split-fold rear seat and a redesigned leather-wrapped Formula steering wheel. Standard S/E suspension included 14x7 in. aluminum wheels.

Standard on the Trans Am was the 5.0 liter V-8 which gained additional horsepower from the 1982 version. The T5 transmission, too, was standard. The Trans Am also got a new hood with an off-center hood bulge that accommodated the new fresh air induction system.

The optional automatic transmission was a four-speed unit that featured a lockup torque converter. Initially available with the V-8s, it was later made available on all other Firebird engines.

A third V-8 was made available on the Trans Am. This was the same 5.0 liter HO that the Camaro got in April. With the use of a better camshaft and a Rochester Quadrajet carburetor, the HO put out 190 hp, which was 25 hp more than the TBI version produced. The axle ratio with the 5.0 liter HO was 3.73:1, and the WS6 suspension package was included. The only transmission was the five-speed manual.

Only 662 of the 1983 Firebirds got the L69 HO V-8.

California-bound Trans Ams were available only with the 5.0 liter 145 hp four-barrel and automatic transmission.

The finned turbo 15x7 in. wheels were a no-cost option on the Trans Am and S/E.

Pontiac continued to pump out the Special Edition models in 1983. The first was the Twenty-fifth Anniversary Daytona 500

Limited Edition Trans Am. It featured a two-tone white-and-gray paint treatment, an Aero Package and complementary graphics. In the interior, leather Recaro seats, red instrument panel lighting, cruise control, Daytona 500 mats and many other features finished off the package. A total of 2,500 units were scheduled for production.

The Special Edition Recaro Trans Am came with a black-and-gold paint treatment, gold finned turbo cast-aluminum wheels, T-tops, Recaro identification and a gold hood appliqué. In the interior, fully adjustable Recaro seats were finished in leather. Either V-8 was available and the WS6 package was standard.

*1983 Firebird*

# Chapter 18

# 1984 Firebird

## Production

| | |
|---|---|
| 2 dr base | 62,621 |
| 2 dr S/E | 10,309 |
| 2 dr Trans Am | 55,374 |
| Total | 128,304 |

## Serial Numbers

**Description**

1G2AW87H1EN100001
1—United States
G—General Motors
2—Pontiac
A—restraint type (A = manual belts)
W—Firebird body series (S = base, W = Trans Am, X = S/E)
87—body style (87 = 2 dr coupe)
H—engine code
1—check digit, which varies
E—model year (E = 1984)
N—assembly plant (N = Norwood, L = Van Nuys)
100001—consecutive sequence number

**Location**

On plate attached to left side of dash, visible through windshield.

## Engine VIN Codes

F—2.5 L I-4           H—5.0 L V-8 (LG4)
2—2.5 L I-4           G—5.0 L V-8 (L69)
I—2.8 L V-6

## Engine Identification Codes

C4A, C4B, C4C, C4D, C4W, SDA, SDH, SDJ, SDN, SDR, SDS, SDU—
5.0 L V-8 4 bbl 150 hp manual or automatic
SUF, SUH, SUJ, SXA—5.0 L V-8 TBI 190 hp manual or automatic

## Interior Trim Codes

| | | | |
|---|---|---|---|
| Charcoal | 17 | Medium Doeskin | 64 |
| Royal Blue | 22 | Dark Briar Brown | 67 |
| Light Sand Gray | 60 | | |

## Exterior Color Codes

| | | | |
|---|---|---|---|
| White | 11 | Light Royal Blue Metallic | 22 |
| Silver Sand Metallic | 15 | Medium Dark Royal Blue | |
| Black | 19 | Metallic | 27 |

| | | |
|---|---|---|
| Beige | 59 | Spectra Red 75 |
| Light Briar Brown Metallic | 62 | Midnight Sand Gray |
| Dark Gold Metallic | 65 | Metallic 82 |
| Dark Briar Brown Metallic | 67 | |

## Options

| UPC | Description | Retail Price |
|---|---|---|
| | 2 dr coupe 4 & 6 cyl | $8,349.00 & $8,724.00 |
| | 2 dr coupe S/E 6 & 8 cyl | 10,649.00 & 10,849.00 |
| | 2 dr Trans Am | 10,699.00 |
| AC3 | 6 way power driver's seat | 215.00 |
| AK1 | Color-keyed seatbelts | 26.00 |
| AR9 | Bucket seats | 30.00 |
| AU3 | Power door locks | 125.00 |
| A01 | Soft-Ray glass, all windows | 110.00 |
| A31 | Power windows | 185.00–215.00 |
| A90 | Remote control deck lid release | 40.00 |
| BS1 | Added acoustical insulation | 40.00 |
| BX5 | Roof drip moldings | 29.00 |
| B20 | Luxury Trim Group | |
| | Luxury reclining bucket seats | 349.00–359.00 |
| | Lear-Siegler adjustable bucket seats | 400.00–759.00 |
| | Lear-Siegler adjustable bucket seats w/leather trim | 945.00–1,304.00 |
| B34 | Carpeted front floor mats | 20.00 |
| B35 | Carpeted rear floor mats | 15.00 |
| B48 | Luggage compartment trim | 123.00 |
| B57 | Custom Exterior Group | 51.00–112.00 |
| B80 | Roof drip moldings | 61.00 |
| B84 | Vinyl bodyside moldings | 55.00 |
| B91 | Door edge guards | 15.00 |
| B93 | Bright door edge guards (base wo/W51) | 15.00 |
| CC1 | Locking hatch roof w/removable glass panels | 850.00 |
| CD4 | Controlled-cycle windshield wiper system | 50.00 |
| C25 | Rear window wiper-washer system | 120.00 |
| C49 | Electric rear window defogger | 140.00 |
| C60 | AC | 730.00 |
| C95 | Dome reading lamp | 23.00 |
| DE1 | Hinge-mounted louvered rear window sunshield | 210.00 |
| DG7 | LH & RH sport electric OSRV mirrors | 91.00–139.00 |
| DX1 | Hood appliqué | 38.00 |
| D34 | RH visor vanity mirror | 7.00 |
| D35 | Sport OSRV mirrors | 53.00 |
| D42 | Cargo security screen | 69.00 |
| D80 | Rear deck spoiler | 70.00 |
| D84 | Two-tone paint | 205.00 |
| D98 | Vinyl sport stripes | 75.00 |
| G80 | Limited-slip differential axle | 95.00 |
| J65 | Front & rear power disc brakes | 179.00 |
| K05 | Engine block heater | 18.00 |

| UPC | Description | Retail Price |
|---|---|---|
| K22 | HD 94 amp generator | 25.00 |
| K34 | Cruise control w/resume & accelerate features | 175.00 |
| K64 | HD 78 amp generator | 25.00–51.00 |
| K81 | HD 66 amp generator | 51.00 |
| LC1 | 2.8 L V–6 2 bbl engine | 250.00 |
| LG4 | 5.0 L V–8 4 bbl engine | 200.00–550.00 |
| LL1 | 2.8 L HO V–6 2 bbl engine | NC |
| LQ9 | 2.5 L EFI 4 cyl engine (S/E; credit) | (350.00) |
| L69 | 5.0 L HO V–8 4 bbl engine | 530.00 |
| MM4 | 4 speed manual transmission | NC |
| MM5 | 5 speed manual transmission | 125.00 |
| MX0 | 4 speed automatic transmission | 525.00 |
| NP5 | Leather Appointment Group | 75.00 |
| N09 | Locking fuel filler door | 11.00 |
| N24 | Finned turbo cast-aluminum wheels | 325.00 |
| N33 | Tilt steering wheel | 110.00 |
| N78 | Deep-dish Hi-Tech turbo wheels | NC |
| N89 | Aero turbo cast-aluminum wheels | NC |
| N91 | Wire wheel covers w/Locking Package | 185.00 |
| PB4 | Wheel Locking Package | 16.00 |
| P02 | 5 port wheel covers | 38.00 |
| P06 | Wheel trim rings | 38.00 |
| QMW | 195/75R14 blackwall steel-belted radial tires | NC |
| QMX | 195/75R14 whitewall steel-belted radial tires | 62.00 |
| QYA | 205/70R14 blackwall steel-belted radial tires | 58.00 |
| QYC | 205/70R14 white-letter steel-belted radial tires | 88.00–146.00 |
| QYH | 215/65R15 white-letter steel-belted radial tires | 92.00 |
| QYZ | 215/65R15 blackwall steel-belted radial tires | NC |
| TR9 | Lamp Group | 34.00 |
| UA1 | HD battery | 26.00 |
| UL1 | AM/FM ETR stereo radio system w/clock | 287.00 |
| UL6 | AM radio system w/clock | 151.00 |
| UP8 | Dual rear speakers | 40.00 |
| UQ7 | Subwoofer speaker system | 150.00 |
| UU6 | AM/FM ETR stereo radio w/cassette, Seek-&-Scan, graphic equalizer & clock | 590.00 |
| UU7 | AM/FM ETR stereo radio system w/cassette clock | 387.00 |
| UU9 | AM/FM ETR stereo radio system | 248.00 |
| U21 | Rally gauge cluster w/tachometer & trip odometer | 150.00 |
| U63 | AM radio system | 112.00 |
| U75 | Power antenna | 60.00 |
| VJ9 | Calif emissions requirements | 99.00 |

| V08 | HD cooling system | 40.00–70.00 |
| WS6 | Special Performance Package | 408.00 |
| WS7 | Special Performance Package | 229.00–612.00 |
| WY5 | Special Performance Package | 134.00–517.00 |
| WY6 | Special Performance Package | 313.00 |
| W51 | Black Appearance Group | 123.00–152.00 |
| W62 | Aero Package | 199.00 |
| Y84 | Special Edition Recaro Trans Am option | 1,621.00 |
| Y99 | Rally tuned suspension | 50.00 |

## Facts

The 1984 Firebirds showed refinement rather than any major change.

The S/E got a new leather-wrapped Formula steering wheel and full gauges.

Engine availability was unchanged, but the 2.8 liter V-6 was uprated to 125 hp. The 5.0 liter HO V-8, introduced in late 1983, was available on the Trans Am with a five-speed manual transmission. Included with the HO on the Trans Am was the WS6 suspension package.

A new option, the W62 Aero Package, was available on the Trans Am. It consisted of a side skirt treatment that extended to the front and rear of the car, painted in a contrasting color. Complementing lower-body fade-away stripes were also included.

The Trans Am no longer used the front fender flare extensions. New wheels on the Trans Am were the 15x7 in. turbo cast-aluminum wheels. Trans Am decals were used on the right rear bumper.

The Y84 Special Edition Recaro option was still available on the Trans Am. It consisted of leather Recaro seats and complementing interior, 15x7 in. gold Aero Tech wheels and gold hood appliqué. The Aero Package was included.

About 1,500 Trans Am Fifteenth Anniversary models were built. All were finished in white with blue striping, blue Trans Am decals on the left front air inlet cover and right rear bumper, and large Trans Am decals in both doors. The hood came with the off-center bulge and a venetian blind decal that incorporated the Firebird bird. The multitone gray interior included the Recaro seats and white leather-wrapped steering wheel, shifter knob and parking brake handle. Removable T-tops were standard.

The engine for the Fifteenth Anniversary was the 5.0 liter 190 hp V-8 teamed to the five-speed manual transmission. Most noticeable were the 16x8 in. white painted turbo aluminum wheels and P245/50R16 Goodyear Eagle GT tires, more commonly known as Gatorbacks because of their unidirectional tread pattern. The standard WS6 suspension got revised settings, and a larger 25 mm rear sway bar was used.

All base and S/E Firebirds got GM's fourth-generation steel-belted radial tires.

Hydraulic linkage was used on the clutch on all manual-transmission-equipped Firebirds.

*1984 Firebird*

# Chapter 19

# 1985 Firebird

## Production

| | |
|---|---|
| 2 dr base | 46,644 |
| 2 dr S/E | 5,208 |
| 2 dr Trans Am | 44,028 |
| Total | 95,880 |

## Serial Numbers

**Description**
1G2FW87H1FN100001
1—United States
G—General Motors
2—Pontiac
F—car line (F = Firebird)
W—Firebird body series (S = base, W = Trans Am, X = S/E)
87—body style (87 = 2 dr coupe)
H—engine code
1—check digit, which varies
F—model year (F = 1985)
N—assembly plant (N = Norwood, L = Van Nuys)
100001—consecutive sequence number

**Location**
On plate attached to left side of dash, visible through windshield.

## Engine VIN Codes

2—2.5 L I-4
2—2.8 L V-6
H—5.0 L V-8 (LG4)
G—5.0 L V-8 (L69)
F—5.0 L V-8 (LB9)

## Engine Identification Codes

C4P, C4R, C7A, C7B, CDD, CDF, CDH, CDJ, CDL, CKA—5.0 L V-8 4 bbl 150 hp manual or automatic
CDK, CDM, CFF, CFH—5.0 L V-8 4 bbl 175 hp manual or automatic
CDN, CDR, CFA, CFB—5.0 L V-8 TPI 190 hp manual or automatic

## Interior Trim Codes

| | |
|---|---|
| Black | 19 |
| Light Saddle | 62 |
| Russet | 68 |
| Dark Carmine | 72 |
| Medium Dark Gray | 82 |

## Exterior Color Codes

| | | | |
|---|---|---|---|
| White | 11 | Bright Blue Metallic | 30 |
| Silver Metallic | 12 | Yellow Gold | 50 |
| Gray Metallic | 15 | Light Chestnut Metallic | 60 |
| Black | 19 | Red-Brown Metallic | 69 |
| Dark Blue | 26 | Blaze Red | 75 |
| | | Dark Red | 78 |

## Options

| UPC | Description | Retail Price |
|---|---|---|
| | 2 dr coupe 4 & 6 cyl | $8,763.00 & $9,013.00 |
| | 2 dr coupe S/E 6 & 8 cyl | 11,063.00 & 11,263.00 |
| | 2 dr coupe Trans Am | 11,113.00 |
| AC3 | 6 way power seat | 225.00 |
| AK1 | Color-keyed seatbelts | 26.00 |
| AR9 | Bucket seats | 30.00 |
| AU3 | Power door locks | 130.00 |
| A01 | Soft-Ray glass, all windows | 115.00 |
| A31 | Power windows | 195.00–225.00 |
| A90 | Remote control deck lid release | 40.00 |
| BS1 | Added acoustical insulation | 40.00 |
| BX5 | Roof drip moldings | 29.00 |
| B20 | Luxury Trim Group | |
| | Luxury reclining bucket seats | 349.00–359.00 |
| | Lear-Siegler adjustable bucket seats w/Pallex cloth trim | 400.00–759.00 |
| | Lear-Siegler adjustable bucket seats w/leather & Pallex trim | 945.00–1,304.00 |
| | Recaro adjustable bucket seats w/Pallex cloth trim | 636.00–995.00 |
| B34 | Carpeted front floor mats | 20.00 |
| B35 | Carpeted rear floor mats | 15.00 |
| B48 | Luggage compartment trim | 48.00 |
| B57 | Custom Exterior Group | 51.00–112.00 |
| B80 | Roof drip moldings | 61.00 |
| B84 | Vinyl bodyside moldings | 55.00 |
| B91 | Door edge guards | 15.00 |
| B93 | Bright door edge guards (base wo/W51) | 15.00 |
| CC1 | Locking hatch roof w/removable glass panels | 875.00 |
| CD4 | Controlled-cycle windshield wiper system | 50.00 |
| C25 | Rear window wiper-washer system | 125.00 |
| C49 | Electric rear window defogger | 145.00 |
| C60 | AC | 750.00 |
| C95 | Dome reading lamp | 23.00 |
| DE1 | Hinge-mounted louvered rear window sunshield | 210.00 |
| DG7 | LH & RH sport electric OSRV mirrors | 91.00–139.00 |
| DK6 | Interior roof console | 50.00 |
| DX1 | Hood appliqué decal | 95.00 |
| D27 | Luggage compartment lockable load floor | 75.00 |
| D34 | RH visor vanity mirror | 7.00 |

| | | |
|---|---|---:|
| D35 | Sport OSRV mirrors | 53.00 |
| D42 | Cargo security screen | 69.00 |
| D80 | Rear deck spoiler | 70.00 |
| D81 | Aero wing rear deck spoiler | 199.00 |
| D84 | Two-tone paint | 205.00 |
| D98 | Vinyl sport stripes | 75.00 |
| G80 | Limited-slip differential axle | 100.00 |
| J65 | 4 wheel power disc brakes | 179.00 |
| K05 | Engine block heater | 18.00 |
| K22 | HD 94 amp generator | 25.00 |
| K34 | Cruise control w/resume & accelerate features | 175.00 |
| K64 | HD 78 amp generator | 25.00 |
| LB8 | 2.8 L EFI V-6 engine | 350.00 |
| LB9 | 5.0 L EFI V-8 engine | 695.00 |
| LG4 | 5.0 L V-8 4 bbl engine | |
| | Base | 650.00 |
| | S/E | 300.00 |
| | Trans Am | NC |
| LQ9 | 2.5 L EFI 4 cyl engine (base) | NC |
| L69 | 5.0 L HO V-8 4 bbl engine | 695.00 |
| MM5 | 5 speed manual transmission | NC |
| MX0 | 4 speed automatic transmission | 425.00 |
| NP5 | Leather-wrapped Formula steering wheel | 75.00 |
| N09 | Locking fuel filler door | 11.00 |
| N24 | 15 in. deep-dish Hi-Tech turbo cast-aluminum wheels | 325.00 |
| N33 | Tilt steering wheel | 115.00 |
| N90 | 15 in. diamond-spoke cast-aluminum wheels | 325.00 |
| N91 | Wire wheel covers w/Locking Package | 199.00 |
| N96 | 16 in. Hi-Tech turbo cast-aluminum wheels | NC |
| PB4 | Wheel Locking Package | 16.00 |
| PE1 | 14 in. diamond-spoke cast-aluminum wheels | 325.00 |
| P02 | 5 port wheel covers | 39.00 |
| P06 | Wheel trim rings | 39.00 |
| QAC | 235/60VR15 blackwall steel-belted radial tires | 177.00 |
| QDZ | 245/50VR16 blackwall steel-belted radial tires | NC |
| QHW | 205/70R14 white-letter steel-belted radial tires | 88.00–146.00 |
| QHX | 205/70R14 blackwall steel-belted radial tires | 58.00 |
| QMW | 195/75R14 blackwall steel-belted radial tires | NC |
| QMX | 195/75R14 whitewall steel-belted radial tires | 62.00 |
| QMY | 195/75R14 white-letter steel-belted radial tires | 84.00 |
| QYH | 215/65R15 white-letter steel-belted radial tires | 92.00–224.00 |

| UPC | Description | Retail Price |
|-----|-------------|-------------:|
| QYZ | 215/65R15 blackwall steel-belted radial tires | 74.00–132.00 |
| TR9 | Lamp Group | 34.00 |
| UA1 | HD battery | 26.00 |
| UK4 | AM/FM ETR stereo radio w/Seek-&-Scan | 168.00 |
| UL5 | AM radio (delete) | (56.00) |
| UM6 | AM/FM ETR stereo radio system w/cassette, Seek-&-Scan, clock | 329.00 |
| UM7 | AM/FM ETR stereo radio w/Seek-&-Scan, clock | 207.00 |
| UQ7 | Subwoofer speaker system | 150.00 |
| UT4 | AM/FM ETR stereo radio system w/cassette, Seek-&-Scan, graphic equalizer, clock, Touch Control | 519.00 |
| UX1 | AM/FM ETR stereo radio system w/cassette, Seek-&-Scan, graphic equalizer, clock | 479.00 |
| U21 | Rally gauge cluster w/tachometer & trip odometer | 150.00 |
| U75 | Power antenna | 65.00 |
| VJ9 | Calif emissions requirements | 99.00 |
| V08 | HD cooling system | 40.00–70.00 |
| WS6 | Special Performance Package | 664.00 |
| W51 | Black Appearance Group | 123.00–152.00 |
| Y99 | Rally tuned suspension | 30.00 |

## Facts

The 1985 Firebird got a restyle, in and out, though the basic body shell was unchanged. New front and rear end treatments resulted in better aerodynamics. The interior was slightly restyled too, with an electronic instrument panel becoming optional.

The Trans Am got the Aero Package as part of its standard equipment. The side skirts and front and rear bumper extensions were larger with a new air-dam-style rear spoiler optional. Trans Am lettering was embossed on the right side of the bumper panel, and in the front, the Trans Am got a new hood with dual louvers and foglamps mounted in the front panel extensions.

Firebird engine availability included the 88 hp four-cylinder and the 2.8 liter multiport injected V-8. Three versions of the Chevrolet small-block were available. The 5.0 liter 155 hp four-barrel was standard on the Trans Am and optional on the S/E and base. Optional on the Trans Am was the 5.0 liter HO, rated at 190 hp, with a new tuned port injection (TPI) version rated at 205 hp. The HO was available only with the five-speed manual transmission, and the TPI engine was available only with the automatic transmission. The Borg-Warner T5 transmission could not handle the TPI's torque.

Standard suspension on the Trans Am was upgraded to 1984 WS6 specifications but without the four-wheel disc brakes. Standard tires were P215/65R15 Goodyear Eagle GTs on 15x7 in. Hi-Tech wheels. Diamond-spoke aluminum wheels were a no-cost option on the S/E and Trans Am.

The Recaro option was no longer available, but Recaro seats were.

The WS6 suspension option got new gas pressure shocks, four-wheel disc brakes, 16x8 in. Hi-Tech wheels and P245/50VR15 Goodyear Eagle GT tires. The WS6 package included 34 mm front and 25 mm rear sway bars.

Single-needle speedometers were used, rather than the previous one that indicated miles per hour and kilometers per hour simultaneously.

Production records indicate that 1,665 Trans Ams were equipped with the L69 5.0 liter 190 hp V-8.

*1985 Firebird Trans Am*

Chapter 20

# 1986 Firebird

## Production
| | |
|---|---|
| 2 dr base | 59,334 |
| 2 dr S/E | 2,259 |
| 2 dr Trans Am | 48,870 |
| Total | 110,463 |

## Serial Numbers
**Description**
1G2FW87H1GN100001
1—United States
G—General Motors
2—Pontiac
F—car line (F = Firebird)
W—Firebird body series (S = base, W = Trans Am, X = S/E)
87—body style (87 = 2 dr coupe)
H—engine code
1—check digit, which varies
G—model year (G = 1986)
N—assembly plant (N = Norwood, L = Van Nuys)
100001—consecutive sequence number

**Location**
On plate attached to left side of dash, visible through windshield.

## Engine VIN Codes
2—2.5 L I-4
5—2.5 L I-4
S—2.8 L V-6
H—5.0 L V-8 (LG4)
G—5.0 L V-8 (L69)
F—5.0 L V-8 (LB9)
8—5.7 L V-8 (L98)

## Engine Identification Codes
C7D, C7H, DD4, DDC, DDD, DFT, DFU—5.0 L V-8 4 bbl 150 hp manual or automatic
DFR, DFS—5.0 L V-8 4 bbl 165 hp manual or automatic
D4C, D4K, DDA, DDH, DDS, DDT, DDX—5.0 L V-8 TPI 190 hp manual or automatic
DKJ, DKK—5.7 L V-8 TPI 230 hp automatic

## Interior Trim Codes
| | |
|---|---|
| Black | 19 |
| Light Saddle | 62 |
| Russet | 68 |
| Dark Carmine | 72 |
| Medium Dark Gray | 82 |

## Exterior Color Codes

| | | | |
|---|---|---|---|
| Silver Metallic | 13 | Champagne Gold Metallic | 60 |
| Bright Blue Metallic | 23 | Russet Metallic | 66 |
| Black Sapphire Metallic | 28 | Midnight Russet Metallic | 68 |
| White | 40 | Flame Red Metallic | 74 |
| Black | 41 | Bright Red | 81 |
| Yellow Gold | 51 | Gunmetal Metallic | 84 |

## Options

| UPC | Description | Retail Price |
|---|---|---|
| | 2 dr coupe 4 cyl | $ 9,279.00 |
| | 2 dr coupe S/E 6 cyl | 11,995.00 |
| | 2 dr coupe Trans Am | 12,395.00 |
| AC3 | 6 way power driver's seat | 225.00 |
| AK1 | Color-keyed seatbelts | 26.00–69.00 |
| AR9 | Bucket seats | 30.00 |
| AU3 | Power door locks | 130.00 |
| A01 | Soft-Ray glass, all windows | 115.00 |
| A31 | Power windows | 195.00–225.00 |
| A90 | Deck lid release | 40.00 |
| BS1 | Added acoustical insulation | 40.00 |
| BX5 | Black moldings (S/E & Trans Am) | 29.00 |
| B20 | Luxury Trim Group | |
| | Luxury reclining bucket seats | 349.00–359.00 |
| | Recaro adjustable bucket seats | 636.00–995.00 |
| B34 | Carpeted front floor mats | 20.00 |
| B35 | Carpeted rear floor mats | 15.00 |
| B48 | Luggage compartment trim | 48.00 |
| B80 | Bright moldings (base) | 61.00 |
| B84 | Vinyl bodyside moldings | 47.00 |
| B91 | Door edge guards | 15.00 |
| CC1 | Locking hatch roof | 875.00 |
| CD4 | Controlled-cycle windshield wiper system | 50.00 |
| C25 | Rear window wiper-washer | 125.00 |
| C49 | Electric rear window defogger | 145.00 |
| C60 | AC | 750.00 |
| C95 | Dome reading lamp | 23.00 |
| DD8 | Automatic day-night inside rearview mirror | 80.00 |
| DE4 | Hatch roof sunshades | 25.00 |
| DG7 | LH & RH sport electric OSRV mirrors | 91.00 |
| DK6 | Interior roof console | 50.00 |
| DX1 | Hood appliqué decal | 95.00 |
| D27 | Luggage compartment lockable load floor | 75.00 |
| D34 | RH visor vanity mirror | 7.00 |
| D42 | Cargo security screen | 69.00 |
| D80 | Rear deck spoiler | 70.00 |
| D81 | Aero wing spoiler (Trans Am) | NC |
| D84 | Two-tone midbody paint | 205.00 |
| G80 | Limited-slip differential axle | 100.00 |
| J65 | 4 wheel power disc brakes | 179.00 |
| K05 | Engine block heater | 18.00 |

| UPC | Description | Retail Price |
|-----|-------------|-------------:|
| K34 | Cruise control w/resume & accelerate features | 175.00 |
| LB8 | 2.8 L EFI V-6 engine (base) | 350.00 |
| LB9 | 5.0 L EFI V-8 engine | 695.00 |
| LG4 | 5.0 L 4 bbl engine | 400.00–750.00 |
| LQ9 | 2.5 L EFI 4 cyl engine (base) | NC |
| L69 | 5.0 L HO V-8 4 bbl engine | 695.00 |
| MM5 | 5 speed manual transmission | NC |
| MX0 | 4 speed automatic transmission | 465.00 |
| NP5 | Leather-wrapped Formula steering wheels | 75.00 |
| N09 | Locking fuel filler door | 11.00 |
| N24 | 15 in. deep-dish Hi-Tech turbo cast-aluminum wheels | 199.00 |
| N33 | Tilt steering wheels | 115.00 |
| N83 | Rally II styled steel wheels w/trim rings | NC |
| N90 | 15 in. diamond-spoke cast-aluminum wheels | 199.00 |
| N96 | 16 in. Hi-Tech turbo cast-aluminum wheels | NC |
| PB4 | Wheel Locking Package | 16.00 |
| PW7 | 16 in. superlight diamond-spoke cast-aluminum wheels | NC |
| QAC | 235/60VR15 blackwall steel-belted radial tires | 177.00 |
| QDZ | 245/50VR16 blackwall steel-belted radial tires | NC |
| QYH | 215/65R15 white-letter steel-belted radial tires | 92.00 |
| QYZ | 215/65R15 blackwall steel-belted radial tires | NC |
| TR9 | Lamp Group | 34.00 |
| UA1 | HD battery | 26.00 |
| UK4 | AM/FM ETR stereo radio system w/Seek-&-Scan | 168.00 |
| UL5 | AM radio (delete) | (56.00) |
| UM6 | AM/FM ETR stereo radio system w/cassette, Seek-&-Scan & clock | 329.00 |
| UM7 | AM/FM ETR stereo radio system w/clock & Seek-&-Scan | 207.00 |
| UQ7 | Subwoofer speaker system | 150.00 |
| UT4 | AM/FM ETR stereo radio system w/cassette, Seek-&-Scan, graphic equalizer, clock & Touch Control | 519.00 |
| UX1 | AM/FM ETR stereo radio system w/cassette, Seek-&-Scan, graphic equalizer & clock | 479.00 |
| U21 | Rally gauge cluster w/tachometer & trip odometer | 150.00 |
| U75 | Power antenna | 65.00 |
| VJ9 | Calif emissions requirements | 99.00 |
| V08 | HD cooling system | 40.00–70.00 |
| WS6 | Special Performance Package | 664.00 |
| WX1 | Two-tone lower accent paint (delete) | NC |

## Facts

The 1986 Firebirds featured new, variation-of-a-theme nose and taillight treatments. The base model got the rear wing spoiler,

Rally II wheels, Rally tuned suspension, new lower body paint treatment, new base seats and the 2.5 liter engine standard.

The Trans Am got a 140 mph speedometer, a new hood bird decal and backlit instrumentation. Backlit instrumentation was standard on all engines except the base four-cylinder. The Trans Am's standard side stripes could be deleted.

Two 5.0 liter V–8 engines were initially available: the standard Trans Am engine, rated at 160 hp (150 hp on the base and Esprit), and the 5.0 liter TPI engine, rated at 190 hp—15 hp less than in 1985.

The L69 HO engine was discontinued because during its two years of production, it suffered from fuel boiling problems. Production records indicate that twenty-six 1986 Trans Am were built with this engine.

The WS6 suspension came with a 36 mm hollow front sway bar. The rear bar was reduced to 24 mm. The standard bar diameters were 34 mm front and 23 mm rear.

Two new features were the power hatch pulldown and electronically controlled rearview mirrors.

All 1986 Firebirds came with a rear-hatch-mounted third brake light.

This was the last year for the S/E model and the four-cylinder engine.

*1986 Firebird*

# Chapter 21

# 1987 Firebird

## Production

| | |
|---|---|
| 2 dr base | 42,552 |
| 2 dr Formula | 13,160 |
| 2 dr Trans Am | 21,779 |
| 2 dr GTA | 11,096 |
| Total | 88,587 |

## Serial Numbers

**Description**
1G2FS81H1HN100001
1—United States
G—General Motors
2—Pontiac
F—car line (F = Firebird)
S—Firebird body series (S = Firebird, W = Trans Am)
8—body style (8 = 2 dr coupe)
1—restraint system (1 = manual belts)
H—engine code
1—check digit, which varies
H—model year (H = 1987)
N—assembly plant (N = Norwood, L = Van Nuys)
100001—consecutive sequence number

**Location**
On plate attached to left side of dash, visible through windshield.

## Engine VIN Codes

S—2.8 L V-6
H—5.0 L V-8 (LG4)
F—5.0 L V-8 (LB9)
8—5.7 L V-8 (L98)

## Engine Identification Codes

C7L, C7M, DFL, SDB—5.0 L V-8 4 bbl 150 hp manual or automatic
D4W, D34, SDD, SDK, SFD, SFS, SRL—5.0 L V-8 TPI 190 hp manual or automatic
SNA, SNJ—5.7 L V-8 TPI 225 hp automatic

## Interior Trim Codes

| | |
|---|---|
| Black | 19 |
| Light Saddle | 62 |
| Dark Carmine | 72 |
| Medium Dark Gray | 82 |

## Exterior Color Codes

| | | | |
|---|---|---|---|
| Silver Metallic | 13 | Champagne Gold Metallic | 60 |
| Bright Blue Metallic | 23 | Midnight Russet Metallic | 68 |
| Black Sapphire Metallic | 28 | Flame Red Metallic | 74 |
| White | 40 | Bright Red | 81 |
| Black | 41 | Gunmetal Metallic | 84 |
| Yellow Gold | 51 | | |

## Options

| UPC | Description | Retail Price |
|---|---|---|
| | 2 dr coupe 6 cyl | $10,359.00 |
| | 2 dr coupe Trans Am | 13,259.00 |
| AH3 | 4 way manual driver's seat adjuster | 35.00 |
| A01 | Tinted glass | 120.00 |
| B2L | 5.7 L FI V-8 engine | 1,045.00 |
| B20 | Custom interior trim | NC |
| B34 | Carpeted front & rear floor mats | 35.00 |
| CC1 | Locking hatch roof | 920.00 |
| C49 | Electric rear window defogger | 145.00 |
| C60 | Electronic AC | 825.00 |
| DG7 | LH & RH sport power remote mirrors | 91.00 |
| DX1 | Hood appliqué decal | 95.00 |
| D42 | Cargo security screen | 69.00 |
| G80 | Limited-slip differential axle | 100.00 |
| J65 | 4 wheel power disc brakes | 179.00 |
| KC4 | Engine oil cooler | 110.00 |
| LB8 | 2.8 L FI V-6 engine | NC |
| LB9 | 5.0 L FI V-8 engine | 745.00 |
| LG4 | 5.0 L V-8 4 bbl engine | 400.00 |
| MM5 | 5 speed manual transmission | NC |
| MX0 | 4 speed automatic transmission | 490.00 |
| NB2 | Calif emissions requirements | 99.00 |
| N24 | 15 in. deep-dish Hi-Tech turbo aluminum wheels | 215.00 |
| N90 | 15 in. diamond-spoke aluminum wheels | 215.00 |
| QDZ | P245/50VR16 blackwall steel-belted radial tires | NC |
| QYH | P215/65R15 white-letter steel-belted radial tires | 102.00 |
| QYZ | P215/65R15 blackwall steel-belted radial tires | NC |
| UA1 | HD battery | 26.00 |
| UL5 | AM radio (delete) | (56.00) |
| UM6 | AM/FM ETR stereo w/cassette & clock | 339.00 |
| UM7 | AM/FM ETR stereo & clock | 217.00 |
| UQ7 | Subwoofer speaker system | 150.00 |
| UT4 | AM/FM ETR stereo w/cassette, graphic equalizer, clock & Touch Control | 529.00 |

| UPC | Description | Retail Price |
|-----|-------------|-------------:|
| UX1 | AM/FM ETR stereo w/cassette, graphic equalizer & clock | 489.00 |
| U21 | Rally cluster gauges w/tachometer & trip odometer | 150.00 |
| U52 | Electronic instrument cluster | 275.00 |
| U75 | Power antenna | 70.00 |
| WS1 | Firebird Performance Value Package #1 | |
| | Base | 265.00 |
| | Trans Am | 839.00 |
| WS3 | Firebird Performance Value Package #2 | 709.00 |
| WS6 | Special Performance Package | 385.00 |
| WX1 | Two-tone lower accent paint (delete) | (150.00) |
| W61 | Firebird Option Group #1 | |
| | Base | 1,273.00 |
| | Formula | 1,273.00 |
| | Trans Am | 1,697.00 |
| | Trans Am GTA | 1,701.00 |
| W63 | Firebird Option Group #2 | |
| | Base | 1,792.00 |
| | Formula | 1,842.00 |
| | Trans Am | 1,949.00 |
| | Trans Am GTA | 1,958.00 |
| W66 | Formula option | 1,070.00 |
| Y84 | GTA option | 2,700.00 |
| Y99 | Rally tuned suspensions | 50.00 |
| — | Custom reclining bucket seats | 319.00–349.00 |
| — | Custom reclining bucket seats w/Pallex cloth w/leather | 619.00–649.00 |
| — | Articulating bucket seats | 619.00–649.00 |

## Facts

Only two Firebird models were available for 1987: the base and the Trans Am. The four-cylinder engine was discontinued, so the 2.8 liter V-6 was the standard engine on the base model, with the carbureted 5.0 liter V-8 optional.

Two option packages highlighted the 1987 Firebird. The first was optional on the base Firebird. Resurrecting the Formula name, Pontiac included all the performance features of the Trans Am in a lighter package. Standard on the Formula was the 5.0 liter 155 hp (165 hp on the Trans Am) V-8 and the five-speed manual transmission. Other standard features included the WS6 suspension package, which featured four-wheel disc brakes, gas-charged shocks, 36 mm front and 24 mm rear sway bars, a 12.7:1 steering ratio and 16x8 in. Hi-Tech wheels. Other optional engines were the 5.0 liter TPI V-8, rated at 205 hp, and the 5.7 liter TPI V-8, rated at 210 hp and available only with the automatic transmission. Formula identification was enhanced by Formula door decals, two-tone paint, a hood bulge and a standard rear spoiler.

The Trans Am got the color-contrasted Aero Package as part of its standard equipment.

More significant was the GTA option package, which consisted of the 5.7 liter TPI V-8, a four-speed automatic and the WS6 suspension package. GTAs got monochromatic paint (one-tone color), GTA nose and fender badges, gold cross-lace 16x8 in. wheels and, in the interior, articulated seats. Also included was the new 140 mph speedometer. The axle ratio was 3.27:1.

Based on the Corvette 5.7 liter V-8, the Firebird's version did not come with aluminum heads or stainless steel headers. Cast-iron heads and exhaust manifolds were used instead.

All V-8s got roller lifters for increased efficiency.

A total 11,380 of the 5.7 liter V-8s were installed in either Formula or GTA Firebirds.

This was the last year the Firebirds were built at the Norwood, Ohio, plant. From 1988, they would be assembled at the Van Nuys plant only.

*1987 Firebird Formula*

# Chapter 22

# 1988 Firebird

## Production

| | |
|---|---|
| 2 dr Firebird | 28,973 |
| 2 dr Formula | 13,475 |
| 2 dr Trans Am | 8,793 |
| 2 dr GTA | 11,214 |
| Total | 62,455 |

## Serial Numbers

**Description**

1G2FS81F1HL100001

1—United States
G—General Motors
2—Pontiac
F—car line (F = Firebird)
S—Firebird body series (S = Firebird, W = Trans Am)
8—body style (8 = 2 dr coupe)
1—restraint system (1 = manual belts)
F—engine code
1—check digit, which varies
H—model year (H = 1988)
L—assembly plant (L = Van Nuys)
100001—consecutive sequence number

**Location**

On plate attached to left side of dash, visible through windshield.

## Engine VIN Codes

S—2.8 L V-6 135 hp
E—5.0 L V-8 150 hp
F—5.0 L V-8 190/215 hp
8—5.7 L V-8 225 hp

## Engine Identification Codes

CJB, CJC—5.0 L V-8 TBI 150 hp manual or automatic
CHA, CHB, CHP—5.0 L V-8 TPI 190 hp manual or automatic
CUA—5.7 L V-8 TPI 225 hp automatic

## Interior Trim Codes

| | |
|---|---|
| Black | 19 |
| Medium Beachwood | 66 |
| Dark Carmine | 72 |
| Medium Dark Gray | 82 |

## Exterior Color Codes

| | |
|---|---|
| Silver Metallic | 13 |
| Blue Metallic | 23 |
| White | 40 |
| Black | 41 |
| Yellow Gold | 51 |
| Orange Metallic | 63 |
| Flame Red Metallic | 74 |
| Bright Red | 81 |
| Gunmetal Metallic | 87 |

# Options

| UPC | Description | Retail Price |
|-----|-------------|--------------|
| | 2 dr coupe Firebird 6 cyl | $10,999.00 |
| | 2 dr coupe Firebird Formula | 11,999.00 |
| | 2 dr coupe Trans Am | 13,999.00 |
| | 2 dr coupe Trans Am GTA | 19,299.00 |
| AQ9 | Luxury articulating bucket seats | 319.00–530.00 |
| AR9 | Custom reclining bucket seats | NC |
| AU3 | Power door locks | 145.00 |
| A31 | Power windows | 240.00 |
| B20 | Luxury interior trim | 293.00 |
| B34 | Front & rear floor mats | 35.00 |
| CC1 | Locking hatch roof | 920.00 |
| C49 | Electric rear window defogger | 145.00 |
| C60 | AC | 895.00 |
| C67 | Electronic AC | 945.00 |
| D42 | Cargo security screen | 69.00 |
| D86 | Deluxe two-tone paint | 150.00 |
| G80 | Limited-slip differential axle | 100.00 |
| J65 | 4 wheel power disc brakes | 179.00 |
| KC4 | Engine oil cooler | 110.00 |
| LB8 | 2.8 L MPFI V-6 engine | NC |
| LB9 | 5.0 L MPFI V-8 engine | 745.00 |
| L03 | 5.0 L TBFI V-8 engine | 400.00 |
| MM5 | 5 speed manual transmission | NC |
| MX0 | 4 speed automatic transmission | 490.00 |
| NB2 | Calif emissions requirements | 99.00 |
| N24 | 15 in. deep-dish Hi-Tech turbo aluminum wheels | NC |
| N90 | 15 in. diamond-spoke aluminum wheels | NC |
| N96 | 16 in. Hi-Tech turbo aluminum wheels | NC |
| PEO | 16 in. deep-dish Hi-Tech turbo aluminum wheels | NC |
| PW7 | 16 in. diamond-spoke aluminum wheels | |
| | Gold | NC |
| | Body color | NC |
| QDZ | P245/50VR16 blackwall steel-belted radial tires | 385.00 |
| QYZ | P215/65R15 blackwall steel-belted radial tires | NC |
| UL5 | AM radio (delete) | (165.00) |
| UM6 | AM/FM ETR stereo w/cassette & clock | 122.00 |
| UM7 | AM/FM ETR stereo & clock | NC |
| UQ7 | Subwoofer speaker system | 150.00 |
| UT4 | AM/FM ETR stereo w/cassette, graphic equalizer, clock & Touch Control | NC |
| UX1 | AM/FM ETR stereo w/cassette, graphic equalizer & clock | 272.00 |
| U52 | Electronic instrument cluster | 275.00 |
| U75 | Power antenna | 70.00 |

| UPC | Description | Retail Price |
|---|---|---|
| WX1 | Two-tone lower accent paint (delete) | (150.00) |
| Y99 | Rally tuned suspension | 50.00 |
| 1SA | Option Group #1 | |
| | Firebird & Formula | 1,093.00 |
| | Trans Am | 1,327.00 |
| 1SB | Option Group #2 | |
| | Firebird & Formula | 1,362.00 |
| | Trans Am | 1,803.00 |
| 1SC | Option Group #3 (Firebird & Formula) | 1,697.00 |
| 19P | 16 in. Black diamond-spoke aluminum | |
| | wheels w/Locking Package | NC |

## Facts

A 120 mph speedometer became standard on the base Firebird, replacing the 85 mph unit. A monotone exterior paint scheme and 15x7 in. Hi-Tech turbo or diamond-spoke aluminum wheels were all standard. Engine availability remained at two: the standard 2.8 liter V-6 or the 5.0 liter 150 hp V-8, which now came with TBI, replacing the previous four barrel carburetor.

The Formula got the 5.0 liter TBI engine standard. Optional was an improved 5.0 liter TPI, which was rated at 190 hp with the four-speed automatic or 215 hp with the five-speed manual. The 5.7 liter V-8 was again optional, rated at 225 hp and mated to the four-speed automatic. The 120 mph speedometer came with the 5.0 liter TBI; a 140 mph unit replaced it with both TPI engines. As before, the Formula included the WS6 package, and in 1988, 16x8 in. Hi-Tech turbo wheels.

On the Trans Am, engines and transmissions paralleled those on the Formula but the WS6 package was an option. The 13x7 in. diamond-spoke wheels were standard on the Trans Am.

The GTA was elevated to top-model status. Besides having the 5.7 liter V-8, automatic transmission, 16x8 in. gold lace wheels and WS6 suspension, the GTA was loaded up with practically every other Firebird option. Air conditioning, rear defogger, power windows and locks, cruise control, tilt wheel, steering wheel radio controls, AM/FM cassette stereo with graphic equalizer, Pass Key antitheft system, articulated seats, 45-45 split folding rear seat, rear deck power pulldown and cloth trim or optional leather were all included.

Optional on the GTA was the 5.0 liter TPI V-8.

LCD instrumentation was optional on the GTA and Trans Am.

Silver Blue and Medium Orange paint were highlighted on the Formula.

All V-8 engines got a serpentine accessory drive belt system and valvetrain modifications. The fuel injection systems were also improved.

An engine oil cooler was required with the 5.7 liter V-8.

The redesigned steering wheel featured four spokes.

Camel was a new cloth interior color.

All Firebirds were built at the Los Angeles Van Nuys plant.

*1988 Firebird Formula*

# Chapter 23

# 1989 Firebird

## Production

| | |
|---|---|
| 2 dr Firebird | 32,376 |
| 2 dr Formula | 16,670 |
| 2 dr Trans Am | 5,727 |
| 2 dr GTA | 9,631 |
| Total | 64,404 |

## Serial Numbers

**Description**

1G2FS81F1KL100001

1—United States
G—General Motors
2—Pontiac
F—car line (F = Firebird)
S—Firebird body series (S = Firebird, W = Trans Am)
8—body style (8 = 2 dr coupe)
1—restraint system (1 = manual belts)
F—engine code
1—check digit, which varies
K—model year (H = 1989)
L—assembly plant (L = Van Nuys)
100001—consecutive sequence number

**Location**

On plate attached to left side of dash, visible through windshield.

## Engine VIN Codes

| | |
|---|---|
| 7—2.8 L V-6 135 hp | F—5.0 L V-8 190/215 hp |
| E—5.0 L V-8 170 hp | 8—5.7 L V-8 225 hp |

## Engine Identification Codes

AKH, AKJ—5.0 L V-8 TBI 170 hp manual or automatic
ATA, ATB, ATF, ATM—5.0 L V-8 TPI 190 hp manual or automatic
AWA, AWK—5.7 L V-8 TPI 225 hp automatic

## Exterior Color Codes

| | |
|---|---|
| Blue Metallic | 23 |
| White | 40 |
| Black | 41 |
| Flame Red Metallic | 74 |
| Bright Red | 81 |
| Gunmetal Metallic | 87 |
| Bright Blue Metallic | 98 |

## Interior Trim Codes

| | |
|---|---|
| Black | 19 |
| Medium Beachwood | 66 |
| Medium Dark Gray | 82 |

# Options

| UPC | Description | Retail Price |
|-----|-------------|-------------|
| | 2 dr coupe Firebird | $12,438.00 |
| | 2 dr coupe Firebird Formula | 14,388.00 |
| | 2 dr coupe Trans Am | 16,438.00 |
| | 2 dr coupe Trans Am GTA | 20,778.00 |
| AH3 | 4 way manual driver's seat adjuster | 35.00 |
| AQ9 | Luxury articulating bucket seats | 450.00 |
| AR9 | Custom reclining bucket seat | NC |
| AU3 | Power door locks | 155.00 |
| A31 | Power windows | 250.00 |
| A90 | Remote deck lid release | 50.00 |
| B20 | Luxury interior trim | 293.00 |
| B84 | Bodyside moldings | 60.00 |
| B2L | 5.7 L MPFI V-8 engine | 1,045.00 |
| CC1 | Locking hatch roof | 920.00 |
| C49 | Electric rear window defogger | 150.00 |
| C60 | Custom AC | 795.00 |
| DC4 | Inside rearview mirror w/dual reading lamps | 23.00 |
| DG7 | LH & RH sport power mirrors | 91.00 |
| D42 | Cargo security screen | 69.00 |
| D86 | Deluxe two-tone paint | 150.00 |
| G80 | Limited-slip differential axle | 100.00 |
| J65 | 4 wheel power disc brakes | 179.00 |
| KC4 | Engine oil cooler | 110.00 |
| K34 | Cruise control | 185.00 |
| LB8 | 2.8 L MPFI V-6 engine | NC |
| LB9 | 5.0 L MPFI V-8 engine | 745.00 |
| L03 | 5.0 L TBFI V-8 engine | 400.00 |
| MM5 | 5 speed manual transmission | NC |
| MX0 | 4 speed automatic transmission | 515.00 |
| NB2 | Calif emissions requirements | 100.00 |
| N10 | Dual converter exhaust | 155.00 |
| N24 | 15 in. charcoal deep-dish Hi-Tech turbo aluminum wheels | NC |
| PE0 | 16 in. deep-dish Hi-Tech turbo aluminum wheels | NC |
| PW7 | 16 in. diamond-spoke aluminum wheels | NC |
| QLC | High-performance P245/50ZR16 blackwall steel-belted radial tires | 385.00 |
| QNS | Performance P215/65R15 blackwall steel-belted radial tires | NC |
| QPH | Touring P215/65R15 blackwall steel-belted radial tires | NC |
| TR9 | Lamp Group | 34.00 |
| UM6 | AM/FM ETR stereo w/cassette & clock | 132.00 |
| UM7 | AM/FM ETR stereo & clock | NC |
| UT4 | AM/FM ETR stereo w/cassette, graphic equalizer, clock & Touch Control | 317.00–447.00 |

| UPC | Description | Retail Price |
|-----|-------------|-------------:|
| UX1 | AM/FM ETR stereo w/cassette, graphic equalizer & clock | 150.00–282.00 |
| U75 | Power antenna | 70.00 |
| U1A | AM/FM stereo w/compact disc player, clock & graphic equalizer | 79.00–526.00 |
| WX1 | Two-tone lower accent paint (delete) | (150.00) |
| W68 | Sport Appearance Package | 450.00 |

## Facts

The model line-up in 1989 was unchanged from that in 1988.

The 5.0 liter TBI was uprated to 170 hp. Air conditioning was standard equipment with this engine. The 5.7 liter engine got an exhaust system with a dual catalytic converter for a 10 hp increase on the Formula model.

The Formula got a narrower side stripe. Engine and suspension options were unchanged.

Improvements included a revised electric rear hatch lid, new three-point rear lap and shoulder belts, and new calipers and rotors on the rear disc brakes. The Pass Key antitheft system was now standard on all Firebirds.

The N10 dual converter exhaust system was required with the 5.0 liter TPI and manual transmission and on the 5.7 liter V-8 powered GTA.

Available only on the GTA was a fiberglass notchback hatch lid.

The W68 Sport Appearance Package, available on the Firebird, included the Trans Am Aero front and rear bumper extensions, foglamps and moldings and required the 5.0 liter TBI V-8.

A total 1,500 Twentieth Anniversary Trans Am models were built, powered with the Buick 3.8 liter 245 hp Turbo V-6, mated to the four-speed automatic. The color was white with a camel interior. The GTA script on the fenders was changed to Turbo Trans Am and the GTA emblem on the nose was changed to a Twentieth Anniversary insignia. The same insignia was used on the sail panels.

*1989 Firebird Formula*

# Chapter 24

# 1990 Firebird

## Production

| | |
|---|---|
| 2 dr Firebird | 13,204 |
| 2 dr Formula | 4,832 |
| 2 dr Trans Am | 1,054 |
| 2 dr GTA | 1,442 |
| Total | 20,532 |

## Serial Numbers

**Description**
1G2FS83F1LL100001
1—United States
G—General Motors
2—Pontiac
F—car line (F = Firebird)
S—Firebird body series (S = Firebird, W = Trans Am)
8—body style (8 = 2 dr coupe)
3—restraint system (3 = manual belts, driver's-side air bag)
F—engine code
1—check digit, which varies
L—model year (L = 1990)
L—assembly plant (L = Van Nuys)
100001—consecutive sequence number

**Location**
On plate attached to left side of dash, visible through windshield.

## Engine VIN Codes

| | |
|---|---|
| T—3.1 L V-6 135 hp | F—5.0 L V-8 190/215 hp |
| E—5.0 L V-8 170 hp | 8—5.7 L V-8 235 hp |

## Engine Identification Codes
BLC, BLD—5.0 L V-8 TBI 170 hp manual or automatic
BLF, BLH, BLJ—5.0 L V-8 TPI 190 hp manual or automatic
BMK—5.7 L V-8 TPI 235 hp automatic

## Exterior Color Codes

| | |
|---|---|
| Silver Blue Metallic | 23 |
| Black | 41 |
| Brilliant Red Metallic | 75 |
| Bright Red | 81 |
| Medium Gray Metallic | 87 |
| Bright Blue Metallic | 98 |

## Interior Trim Codes

| | |
|---|---|
| Black | 19 |
| Medium Beachwood | 66 |
| Medium Dark Gray | 82 |

# Option

| UPC | Description | Retail Price |
|---|---|---|
| | 2 dr coupe Firebird | $11,759.00 |
| | 2 dr coupe Firebird Formula | 15,049.00 |
| | 2 dr coupe Trans Am | 16,949.00 |
| | 2 dr coupe Trans Am GTA | 23,759.00 |
| AH3 | 4 way manual driver's seat adjuster | 35.00 |
| AQ9 | Luxury articulating bucket seats | 450.00 |
| AR9 | Custom reclining bucket seats | NC |
| AU3 | Power door locks | 175.00 |
| A31 | Power windows | 260.00 |
| A90 | Remote deck lid release | 50.00 |
| B84 | Bodyside moldings | 60.00 |
| B2L | 5.7 L MPFI V–8 engine | 745.00 |
| CC1 | Locking hatch roof | 920.00 |
| C49 | Electric rear window defogger | 160.00 |
| C60 | Custom AC | 805.00 |
| DC4 | Inside rearview mirror w/dual reading lamps | 23.00 |
| DG7 | LH & RH sport power mirrors | 91.00 |
| D42 | Cargo security screen | 69.00 |
| D86 | Deluxe two-tone paint | 150.00 |
| G80 | Limited-slip differential axle | 100.00 |
| J65 | 4 wheel power disc brakes | 179.00 |
| KC4 | Engine oil cooler | 110.00 |
| K34 | Cruise control | 195.00 |
| LB9 | 5.0 L MPFI V–8 engine | 745.00 |
| LH0 | 3.1 L MPFI V–6 engine | NC |
| L03 | 5.0 L TBFI V–8 engine | 350.00 |
| MM5 | 5 speed manual transmission | NC |
| MX0 | 4 speed automatic transmission | 515.00 |
| NB2 | Calif emissions requirements | 100.00 |
| N10 | Dual converter exhaust | 155.00 |
| N24 | 15 in. charcoal deep-dish Hi-Tech turbo aluminum wheels | NC |
| PE0 | 16 in. deep-dish Hi-Tech turbo aluminum wheels w/Locking Package | NC |
| PW7 | 16 in. diamond-spoke aluminum wheels | NC |
| QLC | High-performance P245/50ZR16 blackwall steel-belted radial tires | 385.00 |
| QNS | Performance P215/65R15 blackwall steel-belted radial tires | NC |
| QPH | Touring P215/65R15 blackwall steel-belted radial tires | NC |
| UM6 | AM/FM ETR stereo w/cassette & clock | 150.00 |
| UM7 | AM/FM ETR stereo & clock | NC |
| UX1 | AM/FM stereo w/cassette, graphic equalizer & clock | 150.00–300.00 |
| U75 | Power antenna | 75.00 |
| U1A | AM/FM stereo w/compact disc player, clock & graphic equalizer | 226.00–526.00 |
| WDV | NY warranty enhancements | 65.00 |

| WX1 | Two-tone lower accent paint (delete) | (150.00) |
|-----|--------------------------------------|----------|
| W68 | Sport Appearance Package | 450.00 |

## Facts

The 1990 Firebird model run was abbreviated, as the 1991 models were a mid 1990 introduction. The model line up was a carryover from that in 1989. Exterior styling was unchanged, but many mechanical and trim changes were made.

A driver's-side air bag was standard equipment on the Firebird, one of the few GM cars offering the system.

The base Firebird got the 3.1 liter multiport fuel-injected (MPFI) V-6 and 140 hp. The 5.0 liter 170 hp TBI V-8 was optional. The base Firebird's standard wheels were 15x7 in. Hi-Tech bright port turbos faced with charcoal. The base model also got a new rear spoiler.

The Formula got the 5.0 liter TBI standard with the 5.0 liter 220/225 hp TPI and 5.7 liter 240 hp TPI V-8s optional. The Formula also got the Aero rear spoiler without the Trans Am and GTA moldings.

The Trans Am got the 5.0 liter 200 hp TPI V-8 with a single catalytic converter as standard. The 225 hp five-speed manual version was optional, as was the 5.7 liter, now rated at 235 hp thanks to the dual catalytic converter exhaust system. The 5.0 liter 225 hp also got dual exhausts. Standard Trans Am wheels were the Hi-Tech turbos with charcoal faces. On the optional WS6 package, 16x8 in. Hi-Tech turbo wheels in silver or black faces were available. Tires were P245/50ZR16s, good to 154 mph. Leather seats were not available on the Trans Am.

The GTA got the same features and options as in 1989.

All TPI engines got a speed density fuel injection metering system.

All Firebirds got dual body-color sideview mirrors.

In the interior were new dash switches.

*1990 Firebird GTA*

# Chapter 25

# 1991 Firebird

## Serial Numbers

**Description**
1G2FS83F1ML100001
1—United States
G—General Motors
2—Pontiac
F—car line (F = Firebird)
S—Firebird body series (S = Firebird, W = Trans Am)
8—body style (8 = 2 dr coupe)
3—restraint system (3 = manual belts, driver's-side air bag)
F—engine code
1—check digit, which varies
M—model year (M = 1991)
L—assembly plant (L = Van Nuys)
100001—consecutive sequence number

**Location**
On plate attached to left side of dash, visible through windshield.

## Engine VIN Codes
E—3.1 L V-6 135 hp
F—5.0 L V-8 205/225 hp
8—5.7 L V-8 240 hp

## Engine Identification Codes
CKF, CLH, CLJ, CLW—5.0 L V-8 TBI 205 hp manual or automatic
CMB, CMP—5.7 L V-8 TPI 240 hp automatic

## Exterior Color Codes

| | |
|---|---|
| Bright White | 10 |
| Silver Blue Metallic | 23 |
| Black | 41 |
| Brilliant Red Metallic | 75 |
| Bright Red | 81 |
| Medium Gray Metallic | 87 |
| Bright Blue Metallic | 98 |
| Dark Green Metallic | 45 |

## Interior Trim Codes

| | |
|---|---|
| Black | 19 |
| Medium Beachwood | 66 |
| Medium Dark Gray | 82 |

## Options

| UPC | Description | Retail Price |
|---|---|---|
| | Firebird convertible | 19,159.00 |
| | Trans Am convertible | 22,980.00 |
| | 2 dr coupe Firebird | $12,444.00 |
| | 2 dr coupe Firebird Formula | 15,069.00 |

| | | |
|---|---|---:|
| | 2 dr coupe Trans Am | 17,191.00 |
| | 2 dr coupe Trans Am GTA | 23,934.00 |
| AH3 | 4 way manual driver's seat adjuster | 35.00 |
| AQ9 | Luxury articulating bucket seats | 450.00 |
| AR9 | Custom reclining bucket seats | NC |
| AU3 | Power door locks | 175.00 |
| A31 | Power windows | 260.00 |
| A90 | Remote deck lid release | 50.00 |
| B84 | Bodyside moldings | 60.00 |
| B2L | 5.7 L MPFI V–8 engine | 300.00–1,045.00 |
| CC1 | Locking hatch roof | 920.00 |
| C49 | Electric rear window defogger | 160.00 |
| C60 | Custom AC | 805.00 |
| DC4 | Inside rearview mirror w/flood lamp | 23.00 |
| DG7 | LH & RH sport power mirrors | 91.00 |
| D42 | Cargo security screen | 69.00 |
| GU6 | Performance Enhancement Group | 444.00 |
| G80 | Limited-slip differential axle | 100.00 |
| K34 | Cruise control | 195.00 |
| LB9 | 5.0 L MPFI V–8 engine | 745.00 |
| LH0 | 3.1 L MPFI V–6 engine | 350.00 |
| L03 | 5.0 L TBFI V–8 engine | 350.00 |
| MM5 | 5 speed manual transmission | NC |
| MX0 | 4 speed automatic transmission | 515.00 |
| NB2 | Calif emissions requirements | 100.00 |
| N24 | 15 in. charcoal deep-dish Hi-Tech turbo aluminum wheels w/Locking Package | NC |
| PE0 | 16 in. deep-dish Hi-Tech turbo aluminum wheels w/Locking Package | NC |
| PW7 | 16 in. diamond-spoke aluminum wheels | NC |
| QLC | High-performance P245/50ZR16 blackwall steel-belted radial tires | 313.00 |
| QPE | Touring P215/60R16 blackwall steel-belted radial tires | NC |
| QPH | Touring P215/65R15 blackwall steel-belted radial tires | NC |
| UM6 | AM/FM ETR stereo w/cassette & clock | NC |
| UX1 | AM/FM stereo w/cassette, graphic equalizer & clock | 150.00 |
| U75 | Power antenna | 75.00 |
| U1A | AM/FM stereo w/compact disc player, clock & graphic equalizer | 226.00–376.00 |
| WDV | NY warranty enhancements | 65.00 |
| W68 | Sport Appearance Package | 450.00 |

## Facts

All Firebirds got new front and rear bumper extensions for a new look. All models, except the base, got a new rear deck lid spoiler. Also new was the Trans Am and GTA Aero treatment.

Engine and transmission availability was unchanged from that in 1990, but the horsepower rating on the 5.0 liter TPI automatic equipped engine was raised by 5. The 5.7 liter V-8's rating was also raised by 5 hp to 240 hp.

The T-top hatch roof was not available with the 5.7 liter engine. Tires on the Trans Am were Touring P215/60R15 tires.

The Formula Firebird got a monotone paint treatment.

Required with the 5.7 liter V-8 and 5.0 liter 225 hp TPI V-8 was the GU6 Performance Enhancement Group. It included the N10 dual converter exhaust system, four-wheel disc brakes, engine oil cooler and performance axle ratio.

The W68 Sport Appearance Package was still available on the base Firebird model, simulating the Trans Am look.

A midyear introduction was a convertible available as a base Firebird or a Trans Am. Tops were available in black or beige. Engine & transmission availability is the same as the coupe. The Aero Package was standard with both convertibles. On the Trans Am convertible, the hood has functional hood louvers and air extractors.

*1991 Firebird Trans Am*

*1991 Firebird Trans Am Convertible*

# Appendix

## Engine Identification

Every Pontiac engine has a number stamped on it to identify it and connect it with the car it is installed in. This number consists of the engine code and part of the vehicle's identification number.

The engine code usually consists of two letters and is stamped on a pad on the front of the cylinder block below the right cylinder head. Oldsmobile and Buick V-8 engines that were used on second-generation Firebirds have their codes in the same location. Chevrolet V-8s and Buick V-6s have their codes on a pad in front of the right valve cover, right about where the cylinder head and block meet. Chevrolet engines from 1970 used a three-letter code. Most of these codes are included in the chapters of this book.

Also on the pad may be found the last six or eight digits of the car's VIN. This ties in the installed engine with the chassis.

## Engine Casting Date Codes

Although it is beyond the scope of this book to list all engine part casting numbers, it is useful to be able to decode the date a part was cast. Most parts used on an engine should predate the assembly date code of the engine and should be within thirty days of engine assembly. Exceptions do exist, such as parts cast for use at a later date or model year. A good example is the last batch of 400 ci engines built in 1978 and stored for use on 1979 models.

Engine casting date codes consist of three or four digits. The first digit is a letter that stands for the month, beginning with A for January and ending with L for December. The next number stands for the date of the month, and the last number stands for the last number of the model year. For example, B228 stands for February 22, 1968.

The date code is located on the right (passenger's-side) rear on six-cylinder and small-block Chevrolet V-8s; on big-block Pontiac V-8s, it is stamped on the distributor pad.

In much the same way, subsidiary parts, such as manifolds, carry a similar casting date.

Casting numbers for Pontiac cylinder heads are included in each chapter of this book. The number listed is usually two or three digits. This is not the full casting number, but rather the last two or three digits. For example, the full casting number for the 1969 Ram Air IV engine is 9796722; in the 1969 Firebird chapter, you'll find the number 722 listed. On most Pontiac cylinder heads, these numbers are cast just above the center exhaust ports, thus making identification relatively easy. Remember, too, that the casting number is *not* the same as the cylinder head's part number. Sometimes the cylinder head part number and casting number may be the same; most often they are not.

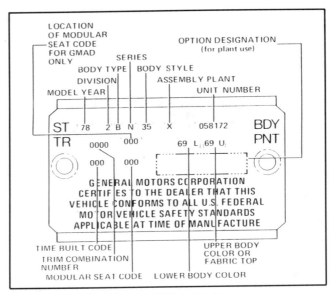

*Typical Firebird cowl tag. A 1978 tag is shown.*

## Cowl Tags

An important way to identify a Firebird is by the cowl tag. This is a thin sheet metal tag with stamped numbers and letters that is riveted on the left side of the cowl in the engine compartment.

The 1967 Firebirds use a plate that deciphers as follows:

Line 1    The time built code, which consists of two numbers followed by a letter. The numbers—ranging from 01 to 12—represent the months of the year. The letters—A, B, C, D, E—represent the first through the fifth weeks of production. For example, time built code 03C would decode to the third production week of March.

Line 2    A long number that starts with the model year, represented by the last two digits of the model year. This is followed by the division series and body series, which must match the first five digits of the car's VIN. The following three letters represent the assembly plant at which the vehicle was built. The final six numbers are the consecutive sequence number, which must match the one on the car's VIN.

Line 3    The car's trim number and color. This line includes codes for vinyl roof and convertible top colors, if so equipped. These codes are included in each chapter of this book.

The plate used from 1968 on was slightly redesigned. The time built code was relocated on a third line, which was followed by a modular seat code. The modular seat code was the RPO code for the type of seat the car was equipped with.

The 1983-91 Firebirds did not use a cowl tag. Instead, a body number plate was located on the upper horizontal surface of the shroud in front of the radiator. The information recorded on the plate was the model year, car division, series, style, body assembly plant, body number, trim combination, modular seat code, paint code and build date. Noted in the GM parts catalog is a warning that beginning with the 1985 model year, this plate may not be on every vehicle. These cars also came with an option label located in the console, listing all the options the car was built with in addition to engine and transmission type.

## Certification Labels

Beginning with 1968, all Pontiac vehicles included a certification label attached on the inside face of the driver's door. The label stated that the vehicle conformed to all applicable safety standards. In addition, the label contained the month and year the vehicle was built along with its VIN. This label was revised in the late seventies and eighties, to contain additional information such as vehicle weight ratings.

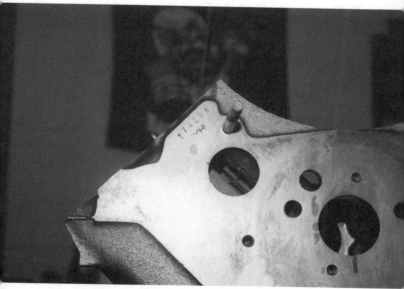

*Pontiac engine code location.* Bart Orlans